Historical Association Studies

Revolution and Counter-Revolution in France 1815–1852

D1410507

Historical Association Studies
General Editors: M.E. Chamberlain and James Shields

The Historical Association, 59a Kennington Park Road.
London SE11 4JH

Revolution and Counter-Revolution in France 1815–1852

WILLIAM FORTESCUE

Basil Blackwell

First published 1988

Basil Blackwell Ltd
108 Cowley Road, Oxford, 0X4 1JF, UK

Basil Blackwell Inc.
432 Park Avenue South, Suite 1503
New York, NY 10016, USA

British Library Cataloguing in Publication Data
Fortescue, William
    Revolution and counter-revolution in
    France 1815–1852 — (Historical Association
    studies)
    1. France. Political events, 1815–1852
    I. Title   II. Series
    944.06

    ISBN   0–631–14515–X

Library of Congress Cataloging in Publication Data
Fortescue, William, 1945–
    Revolution and counter-revolution in France, 1815–1852 / William
Fortescue.
        p.   cm. — (Historical Association studies)
    Bibliography: p.
    Includes index.
    ISBN 0–631–14515–X (pbk.)
    1. France—History—Restoration, 1814–1830. 2. France—History
—Louis Philip, 1830–1848. 3. France—History—Second Republic,
1848–1852. I. Title.   II. Series
DC256.F67   1988
944.06—dc19   88–10520
                                                                     CIP

Typeset in 9.5 on 10 point Baskerville by Photo·Graphics, Honiton.
Printed in Great Britain by *Billing & Sons Ltd, Worcester*

Contents

1 The Restoration of the Bourbon Monarchy, 1814–1815

The years 1814 and 1815 were a watershed in the history of France. They finally marked the end of Napoleonic rule in France, of French domination over much of Continental Europe, and of French involvement in a series of wars which had lasted virtually without interruption for some twenty-three years. They also marked the beginning of a new era, in which members of the Bourbon dynasty ruled France as constitutional monarchs with the assistance of a small land-owning élite, Britain enjoyed a maritime and economic supremacy in Western Europe and in many other parts of the world, and peace and even diplomatic co-operation prevailed among the major European powers. Diplomatic crises, minor wars, popular movements and political revolts periodically challenged the 1815 settlement in France and in Europe, notably during 1830 and 1831, when a revolution changed the monarch in France, Belgium separated from the United Netherlands, and a variety of risings and protests flared up across Europe. Nevertheless, the era really began to come to an end only in 1848, with the February Revolution in France resulting in the overthrow of the constitutional monarchy and the proclamation of the Second Republic, and with most European governments being threatened by revolutionary and nationalist movements. However, by the end of the summer of 1849 conservative forces throughout Europe had triumphed. In France this triumph took the form of an astonishing Bonapartist revival: in December 1848 Louis Napoleon Bonaparte, a nephew of the Emperor Napoleon, crushingly defeated his rivals in an election for the presidency of the Republic; and the Prince-President proceeded, with remarkable speed and success, to overcome his opponents through a mixture of political manipulation and repression, to secure his personal retention of power by overthrowing the constitution with a military *coup d'état* in December 1851, and to re-establish a year later the imperial structures and trappings of a Napoleonic régime. Between 1815 and 1852 historical events had apparently come full circle, but in fact the

Second Empire differed significantly from the First, just as the France of 1852 differed significantly from the France of 1815.

Napoleonic rule in France had been a kind of military dictatorship in which large numbers of notables and men of ability could play a prominent role, the whole system being galvanized by Napoleon's extraordinary genius, energy and charisma. Napoleon's achievements as a legislator, administrative reformer and army commander were outstanding, but the Napoleonic system had a number of obvious weaknesses: it owed its continuing prestige and justification to an apparently unending series of successful wars and military campaigns; it required the active support and co-operation of a significant portion of the French élite and at least tacit acceptance by the bulk of the French population; and it depended ultimately on one man – its founder, creator and leader, the Emperor Napoleon himself.

Between 1800 and 1812 Napoleon and his armies won an almost uninterrupted series of military victories. As a result Napoleon was able to create a new Europe, consisting of an expanded French Empire (including Holland, Belgium, territory annexed from various German states and Switzerland, extensive territories around Genoa, Florence and Rome, and the Illyrian provinces along the Adriatic coastline) surrounded by satellite kingdoms (Westphalia, Italy, Naples and Spain) and dependent states (the Grand Duchy of Warsaw, the Confederation of the Rhine, and Switzerland). However, this French-dominated Europe was unacceptable to the other major European powers, Austria, Prussia, Britain and Russia, and they formed a succession of coalitions to fight against Napoleon. While Napoleon's armies repeatedly defeated his Continental opponents, Britain remained relatively immune to French attack, particularly as the French were unable to mount a serious naval challenge after the battle of Trafalgar (1805). Consequently Napoleon attempted to force Britain to capitulate through economic warfare, by excluding all British goods, and goods transported in British ships, from Continental Europe. To be really effective, the Continental System had, like all economic sanctions, to be applied as universally as possible. Britain's enormous importance as a producer of manufactured goods, exporter of colonial products and importer of foodstuffs and raw materials meant that most European states wanted to continue trading with Britain. This was especially true of Portugal and Russia. Napoleon responded with French military occupations of Portugal (1807) and Spain (1808), and by invading Russia at the head of an enormous army in 1812. At last Napoleon had over-reached himself. In the Iberian peninsula French troops became trapped in a wasting guerilla campaign, had to face a British force ably led by the future Duke of Wellington, and sustained the first significant defeat of any French Imperial army at Baylen (1808). Even more devastating, the retreat from Moscow in 1812 shattered the myth of Napoleonic invincibility and largely destroyed an army of over half a million men.

To a much greater extent than the rulers of the other major European states, Napoleon could not trust his own élite or assume acceptance by a majority of his subjects, particularly in the event of a major disaster. King George III suffered from bouts of insanity, the Emperor Francis of Austria was compelled by Napoleon to accept the humiliating treaties of Pressbourg (1805) and Schönbrunn (1809), King Frederick William III of Prussia experienced immediate and total defeat following his ill-judged ultimatum to Napoleon of October 1806, and Tsar Alexander I of Russia had to endure the enormous loss of life and material destruction arising from the invasion of his empire in 1812. Yet not one of these monarchs lost his throne. Having come to power as a result of a political conspiracy and by means of a military *coup d'état*, Napoleon always lacked legitimacy, notwithstanding his· plebiscites, constitutions, coronation in the cathedral of Notre-Dame in the presence of the Pope and eventual marriage to a Habsburg princess. For royalists he remained the usurper who prevented the Bourbon pretender, the Count of Provence, from assuming his lawful inheritance, while for republicans he was the traitor who had overthrown the Republic and betrayed the Revolution. Most members of the wealthy land-owning and official classes were prepared to accept and even to serve him, but only so long as his rule furthered their interests. Napoleon appreciated this, so he tried to secure from members of the élite the loyalty and support which he needed by a lavish distribution of positions, honours and wealth. This policy, however, encouraged not so much devotion to the Emperor as a determination to protect new-found status. The rest of the population of the Empire possessed little power or influence, though the Revolution provided numerous examples of the ferocity and political impact of mob violence. No stranger to mob violence, Napoleon sought general popular approval through a combination of imperial prestige, low taxes and plentiful food supplies. These he could not always guarantee to deliver; and, despite the censorship, police controls and increasingly authoritarian character of his régime, ordinary Frenchmen could respond to apparently unjustified demands and futile wars by evading taxation and conscription, by refusing to obey administrative orders, and even by banditry and criminal violence.

At first Napoleon benefited from a widespread desire in France for peace, stability and efficient government after all the upheavals which had occurred since 1789. Certainly Napoleon's rapid and effective reforms of French legal, institutional and administrative structures, his pacification of the Vendée region of north-western France, his negotiation of a Concordat with the Papacy (1801), and his ending of a decade of international wars by the Treaty of Lunéville (1801) with Austria and the Peace of Amiens (1802) with Britain, all won him popular support and helped to consolidate his régime. The Peace of Amiens lasted barely a year, but the military achievements of the 'Grande Nation', effectively exploited by Napoleonic propaganda, captured the public imagination, while the conquest and occupation of foreign territories created numerous career and economic opportunities. Within France Napoleon was remarkably successful in encouraging notables to rally to his régime and in attracting men of ability to the service of the state. The assumption by Napoleon of the title of Emperor of the French, and his ceremonial coronation in Notre-Dame cathedral (2 December 1804), seemingly further consolidated the new Napoleonic order.

From 1805 to 1808 the Napoleonic Empire enjoyed an unparalleled splendour and success, but thereafter the durability of the régime became ever more uncertain. Relations between Napoleon and the Roman Catholic Church steadily deteriorated after the French annexation of the Papal States and virtual imprisonment of Pope Pius VII in 1809. The consequent gradual breakdown of Church–state relations alienated much of the Catholic Church and many individual Catholics from Napoleon. Similarly, the progressively more authoritarian character of Napoleonic rule antagonized liberals, while the establishment of the Empire and of an imperial nobility, and Napoleon's marriage in 1810 to Marie Louise, daughter of the Emperor of Austria and niece of Queen Marie Antoinette, flagrantly repudiated republican principles. At the same time Napoleon's apparently endless wars meant that the imperial élite became increasingly concerned to defend their positions rather than their Emperor, and that French people generally became increasingly resentful of military conscription, heavy taxation and commercial disruption. The precariousness of the imperial régime was revealed by the Malet conspiracy of October 1812,[1] and was demonstrated again on a much wider scale, and with far more devastating consequences for Napoleon, at the beginning of 1814.

After 1812 Napoleon might have secured the survival of his régime if he had been prepared to abandon the German and Austrian territories which he had annexed and controlled. However, he refused to make any significant concessions to the Allied powers, partly because of a personal psychological inability to capitulate to opponents whom he regarded as his inferiors, partly because he feared that his rule in France would not survive any major humiliation, and partly because he always believed that he could solve his problems by some new military victory. By the beginning of 1814 not even Napoleon's military genius could rescue France from its desperate military situation. Allied armies were invading on all sides, and for the first time in twenty years French civilians experienced the horrors of war. Napoleon's failure either to negotiate a peace settlement or to defeat the foreign invaders revealed the widening gulf between the interests of Napoleon and those of France. The French population, exhausted by decades of war, refused to respond to Napoleon's appeals for resistance against the enemy, while Napoleon's élite, including members of his own family, refused to sacrifice everything in a suicidal last-ditch stand. Consequently Paris, which lacked effective fortifications, was surrendered to the Allies on 31 March 1814 after only a token resistance, thus sparing it the fate suffered by Moscow in 1812.

Confronted by the loss of Paris, the refusal of his marshals to fight another battle, and a decree by the French Senate deposing him (3 April 1814), Napoleon finally recognized the inevitable by signing his formal abdication at Fontainebleau on 6 April 1814. The same day the Senate proclaimed the Count of Provence as King. As late as the beginning of 1814 the chances of the Count of Provence ever succeeding his brother Louis XVI had seemed remote, but Napoleon's refusal to negotiate seriously with the Allies and his military defeat had cost him his throne. The Empress Marie Louise might have ruled as Regent on behalf of her son by Napoleon, the King of Rome (born in March 1811), had not her youth and political inexperience, her lack of support among the Allied governments, and her departure from Paris on Napoleon's orders on 29 March 1814, all counted too heavily against her. Bernadotte, one of Napoleon's marshals and ruler of Sweden since 1810, was proposed as a candidate for the French throne by Tsar Alexander I of Russia but by no one else. Republicanism within France had been crushed by Napoleon and in any case the Allies associated French republicanism with dangerous revolutionary and expansionist forces. That left a Bourbon restoration as the only viable option, especially as the Bourbon cause had suddenly gained new adherents. When British troops entered Bordeaux on 12 March 1814 the municipal authorities adopted the Bourbon colours amidst expressions of popular enthusiasm; a key group of public figures, including Talleyrand and most of Napoleon's marshals, came to see in the recognition of the Count of Provence as King the surest guarantee of their wealth and status; and by the time of Napoleon's abdication the Allied powers viewed a Bourbon restoration as the best means of securing the stability of France and the peace of Europe.

From the beginning of the Bourbon restoration of 1814 the position of the Count of Provence as King was ambiguous. On the one hand he had been called to the throne of his ancestors as the heir to his brother Louis XVI, an hereditary claim to royal sovereignty which he took care to emphasize: he dated the beginning of his reign from 1795, and he officially adopted the title of Louis XVIII, King of France and Navarre. Thus he assumed that Louis XVI's son had briefly reigned as Louis XVII (from Louis XVI's execution on 21 January 1793 until the Prince's death in prison on 8 June 1795), that he had then succeeded, and that he was a traditional ruler of a kingdom rather than a modern-style monarch of a people (such as Napoleon, who had styled himself Emperor of the French). On the other hand, Louis XVIII clearly owed his crown to the Allied defeat of Napoleon and to the backing of influential members of Napoleon's élite; and during his triumphal return to Paris on 2 May 1814 he signed the Proclamation of Saint Ouen in which he committed himself to accepting a two-chamber parliament, a constitutional system, gurantees of essential liberal freedoms, the permanence of the revolutionary land settlement, the maintenance of Napoleonic military ranks and honours, and the recognition of all titles of nobility.

A new constitution, known as the Charter of 1814 and promulgated on 4 June 1814, elaborated the terms of the Proclamation of Saint Ouen. The constitution affirmed the principles of equality before the law, payment of taxes according to wealth rather than status and of equal opportunity in state employment. Essential liberal freedoms were guaranteed, though Roman Catholicism was declared to be the religion of the state. A similar guarantee protected the inviolability of private property. The King acquired extensive powers as head of the executive and a civil list voted at his accession for the duration of his reign, but legislation and taxation required parliamentary consent. Parliament consisted of a Chamber of Peers chosen by the King and a Chamber of Deputies elected by the departments. Prospective parliamentary candidates had to be forty years old and pay annually a thousand francs in direct taxes, while electors had to be thirty years old and pay annually three hundred francs in direct taxes. The King appointed judges, but once appointed they could not be dismissed and the jury system was preserved. Thus the Charter of 1814 confirmed the abolition of the pre-1789 system of privilege, established by the standards of the early nineteenth century a reasonably liberal régime, and set up a constitutional partnership between the monarch and representatives of the land-owning and office-holding élite.

The defeat of Napoleon in 1814 necessitated not just a new régime and constitution for France but also a new international order in Europe. The representatives of the powers which had defeated Napoleon wanted to deprive France of her conquered territories, prevent any resurgence of French expansionism, secure territorial rewards for their own states, and establish a system which would promote European peace and stability. By the First Treaty of Paris, France had to surrender nearly all the Belgian, German, Swiss and Italian territories conquered and annexed since 1792. To check any future expansion of France, relatively strong states were created on France's eastern frontiers: the United Netherlands (Belgium and Holland), Prussia (expanded to include parts of Saxony, Westphalia and the Rhineland), Switzerland (the neutrality of which was guaranteed by international treaty), and Sardinia (Savoy, Piedmont, Genoa and the island of Sardinia). Significant territorial gains were made by Austria, which acquired the provinces of Lombardy and Venetia in northern Italy, Britain, which acquired Heligoland in the North Sea, Malta and the Ionian islands in the Mediterranean, and a string of colonies (the Cape of Good Hope, Ceylon, Mauritius, St Lucia, Trinidad and Tobago), and Russia, which acquired Finland, most of Poland, and Bessarabia at the mouth of the Danube. To encourage stability, all the important European states, with the exception of Switzerland, once again became monarchies. To encourage peace, an attempt was made to achieve a balance of power in Europe; and it was agreed that all future territorial changes in Europe should be sanctioned by meetings or congresses of the great powers.

For France the Treaties of 1814 were not unduly harsh, especially since the French had unleashed twenty years of death and destruction on Europe, and had deposed rulers, annexed territories, exacted indemnities and created new states almost at will. The French retained their 1792 frontiers (with small additions in Savoy and around Philippeville in Belgium) and various colonial enclaves and islands (notably Guadeloupe and Martinique in the West Indies); they did not have to pay an indemnity or suffer foreign military occupation; and they were not even required to return the art treasures they had looted. Napoleon himself was awarded the sovereignty of the island of Elba and an annual pension of two million francs from the French government, while Marie Louise became ruler of the Duchy of Parma. Nevertheless the Treaties of 1814 were widely viewed in France as a national humiliation; and Louis XVIII's acceptance of those Treaties, and the accusation that he owed his throne to French defeats and to the intervention of France's enemies, inevitably counted against him. Also it was unrealistic to have supposed that Napoleon would have found sufficient satisfaction for his restless ambition in ruling the small island of Elba.

While Napoleon began reorganizing Elba with his customary energy and thoroughness, Louis XVIII confronted the much more daunting task of re-establishing the Bourbon monarchy in France. In Louis XVIII's favour were the willingness of most members of the élite to accept and even to serve him, the absence, except in the case of a few army units, of any official or popular resistance to the change of régime, and the legacy of Napoleonic institutions and laws which in effect prepared France for a restoration of the monarchy and which Louis XVIII wisely left unchanged. Louis XVIII himself was quite intelligent, had considerable personal charm, and was willing to salute crowds and common people. Nevertheless, indolent, physically overweight, fifty-nine years old in 1814, and an exile from France for twenty-three years, he could not hope to match Napoleon's charisma or achievements, and he had inherited from Napoleon a divided, exhausted and defeated nation.

So far as the élite was concerned, Louis XVIII tried to win support from representatives of all the main political traditions. Of the seven important government ministers appointed in May 1814, four had served Napoleon, one had presided over the National Assembly during the Revolution and had subsequently worked for Louis XVIII in exile, one belonged to the pre-1789 aristocracy and was the son-in-law of a minister of Louis XVI, and one had joined the aristocratic emigration from revolutionary France in the 1790s. Those awarded peerages and membership of the Chamber of Peers included forty-seven dukes of the pre-1789 nobility, ninety-six former senators and marshals of Napoleon, and six who had been active in the Revolution and six in the Counter-Revolution. Less than half the prefects were replaced (thirty-five out of a total of eighty-seven, of whom five were given alternative posts). Twenty of the new prefects had been Napoleonic functionaries, while twelve had emigrated during the Revolution (four belonged to both categories).

This attempt to achieve a fusion of the different political components of the French élite – pre-1789 aristocracy, royalist émigrés, Napoleonic functionaries and even, in some cases, former republicans – was a sound policy and reasonably successful. However, the upheavals of the preceding twenty-five years had left a legacy of bitter animosities over past political loyalties and behaviour, the status of the titles and honours of the royal and imperial régimes, the permanence of the post-1789 redistribution of land and wealth, and over the continuation of old conflicts between Catholics and Protestants and of more recent divisions within the Catholic Church. Such animosities, conflicts and divisions tended to be fuelled by Louis XVIII's understandable but often tactless desire to honour the traditions and restore the forms of the Bourbon monarchy. The revival of the old court ceremonial, the restoration of Louis XIV's enormous palace at Versailles, the holding of religious services to commemorate royal victims of the Revolution and even would-be assassins of Napoleon, and the translation of the remains of Louis XVI and Marie Antoinette to Saint-Denis in an elaborate ceremony on 21 January 1815 (the anniversary of Louis XVI's execution), all helped to keep the struggles of the past alive and to suggest that a royalist reaction might triumph in the future. Moreover, while many Frenchmen regarded England as the hereditary enemy with which the nation had been almost continuously at war since 1793, for Louis XVIII it was the land which had sheltered him during most of his years of exile and had contributed decisively to his restoration. Hence he invited the Prince Regent to the peace celebrations in Paris, welcomed English visitors at the Tuileries, and maintained close relations with the British ambassador, the Duke of Wellington, all of which tended to outrage Bonapartists and injure French national pride.

Perhaps the most serious weakness of the Restoration Monarchy in 1814–15 was financial. Louis XVIII inherited a depleted treasury, a France virtually reduced to its 1792 frontiers, and a dread of the financial embarrassments that had so plagued Bourbon kings before 1789. Consequently, while scuring from parliament relatively generous financial provision for the royal household, a determination to balance the state budget severely curtailed government expenditure. For the élite this meant a drastic reduction of patronage in the form of official posts and pensions, and for the mass of the population a continuation of Napoleonic taxes when high taxation seemed unjustified and economic circumstances remained difficult. Above all, financial constraints, as well as the end of the Napoleonic Empire and the return of peace, had a devastating impact on the army. Between April and December 1814 the army was reduced from over 530,000 men to about 220,000. The army was further alienated by the re-establishment of privileged regiments to guard the King, by the substituion of the royal Bourbon standard (gold fleurs-de-lys on a white background) for the blue, white and red tricolour as France's national flag, and by the abolition of the privileges and pensions attached to the Legion of Honour, a decoration which the King declined to wear. Nevertheless Louis XVIII enjoyed a singularly crisis-free reign until Napoleon's return from Elba caused the restored Bourbon monarchy to collapse like a house of cards.

Napoleon might have considered himself fortunate to have been granted the sovereignty of Elba, but this was not so. Restless, impulsive and ambitious, he did not possess the right temperament to accept at the age of forty-four a life of semi-retirement as ruler of a small Mediterranean island. Moreover, the French government failed to pay him his promised income; the Emperor of Austria effectively prevented Marie Louise and the King of Rome from joining him in Elba; and there were rumours that the Allies wanted to have him deported to some remote island or even assassinated. Reports of disaffection in the French army, and of growing hostility in France towards Bourbon rule, further encouraged Napoleon to pursue his ambitions again by gambling on his most audacious adventure. Escaping from Elba with just over 1,000 men he landed on the French coast between Fréjus and Antibes on 1 March 1815. Within twenty days he had reached Paris. The 'Flight of the Eagle', as this astonishing achievement came to be known, can be explained in a number of ways. Luck favoured Napoleon, particularly over the failure of a British warship to intercept his small flotilla during the voyage from Elba to France. Napoleon's propaganda, in the form of printed manifestoes and proclamations, skilfully exploited popular nostalgia for the Empire, a widespread sense of injured national pride, and equally widespread fears and grievances associated with Bourbon rule. The news of his landing did not reach Paris until 5 March, when Louis XVIII responded with totally unjustified complacency. Meanwhile Napoleon, as in so many of his military campaigns, took his opponents by surprise by the speed of his advance and by his choice of route (via Gap and Grenoble rather than straight up the Rhône valley). So far as the army was concerned, Napoleon could exploit old loyalties, disaffection with the Bourbons, and the general reluctance of soldiers to fight their former comrades-in-arms and their Emperor.

Army units sent to oppose Napoleon were successfully persuaded to rally to their old commander, while Marshal Ney, who had rashly promised to bring back the usurper to Paris in an iron cage, was soon encouraging his own men to defect. Support also came from much of the civilian population, particularly in the key cities of Grenoble and Lyons, as Napoleon's arrival stimulated a wave of Bonapartist, anti-Bourbon and quasi-revolutionary fervour. In such a confused and rapidly changing situation, it is not surprising that so many officials and notables, uncertain where their loyalties and interests lay, should have accepted and even welcomed Napoleon. Consequently, on 20 March Napoleon re-entered Paris without having encountered any violent resistance against him. Frightened of the prospect of becoming Napoleon's prisoner, and anxious to avoid a civil war, Louis XVIII had abandoned the Tuileries the previous night and fled with a small escort for the comparative security of Belgium.

Two days after regaining Paris Napoleon promulgated a new constitution for France, styled the 'Additional Act to the Constitutions of the Empire'. The constitution was drafted by a committee which included a prominent liberal, Benjamin Constant, so as to win popular support and constitutional legitimacy for Napoleon's rule. This new constitution was strikingly similar to the Charter of 1814, though the qualifications for parliamentary elections were made less restrictive and the freedom of the newspaper press was firmly guaranteed. Napoleon's hostility towards Jacobinism and awareness of the relative weakness of his political position probably encouraged him to reject the options of a revolutionary republic or a personal dictatorship. In the Additional Act he in effect recognized that after all the changes since 1789 a consensus had emerged in France for a constitution which guaranteed individual freedoms, equality before the law and property rights, and which provided the élite with political representation in a national parliament. Approximately one and a half million approved the new constitution in a plebiscite, with about 5,000 against. Support for the Additional Act tended to come from local and government officials and from rural areas where the Revolution had been popular. The very high abstention rate – only about one in five of those eligible bothered to vote – was comparable to that of previous Napoleonic elections and plebiscites, and administrative confusion prevailed in many departments. Elections for a Chamber of Representatives, which replaced the Chamber of Deputies, were held in May, and again the abstention rate was high. The new parliament, consisting of a Chamber of Peers (composed of over a hundred of Napoleon's nominees) and the Chamber of Representatives, met long enough in June to demonstrate its political independence from Napoleon.

Apart from a short-lived attempt by Louis XVIII's niece, the Duchess of Angoulême, to rally the royalists of Bordeaux, active resistance to Napoleon was confined to the Vendée region, where widespread outbreaks of lawlessness under the guise of popular royalism tied down 20,000 troops. However, outside France the representatives of the powers at the Congress of Vienna immediately and unanimously agreed to oppose this second Napoleonic *coup d'état*: they branded Napoleon as 'an enemy and disturber of the peace of the world', and they promised to stay in the field as long as Napoleon remained capable of further mischief. Napoleon himself tried to convince the European states of his peaceful intentions by declaring his recognition of the 1814 peace settlement and by sending emissaries to the Tsar of Russia and the Emperor of Austria, but to no purpose. Napoleon's only hope was to go on the offensive and to administer a crushing defeat on his enemies before they had had time to assemble overwhelmingly superior forces against him. He therefore invaded Belgium with 125,000 men, and on 16 June he forced Allied armies to retreat at engagements at Ligny and Quatre-Bras. Two days later at Waterloo Napoleon failed to break the British infantry squares. The arrival of a Prussian army under Blücher to reinforce the Allies and the failure of another French army under Grouchy to come to Napoleon's aid turned the French retreat into a rout. Napoleon himself managed to dash back to Paris, where he abdicated for the second time on 22 June. Meanwhile the Allied forces advanced on Paris, which surrendered on 4 July.

The collapse of the Restoration Monarchy during the Hundred Days, and the inglorious royal flight to Belgium, obviously constituted formidable blows to Louis XVIII's position and prestige. However, the King had managed to form a government and a court in exile; and his decision to flee to Belgium rather than England meant that he could quickly make for Paris as soon as he had learnt the news of Napoleon's defeat at Waterloo. This laid him open to the accusation that he had returned in the baggage train of France's enemies, but it also meant that he could almost immediately fill the political and constitutional vacuum created by Napoleon's abdication. The King wisely adopted a conciliatory attitude, which was publicly expressed in the Proclamation of Cambrai (28 June); and, as in 1814, influential figures, notably Fouché and Talleyrand, rallied to him after Napoleon's defeat and abdication, while there was again a widespread resurgence of royalist fervour and an even more widespread desire for peace and order.

The circumstances of Louis XVIII's restoration in 1815 nevertheless differed markedly from those which had prevailed in 1814. After Waterloo the Allies treated France as an enemy country. The Austrians and Prussians, in particular, sought revenge for what Napoleon had done to them and for French support for Napoleon and for his renewed military aggression during the Hundred Days: many of their soldiers behaved brutally and rapaciously in France, while Blücher even wanted to blow up a bridge in Paris named after Napoleon's victory over the Prussians at Jena. The bridge survived

11

but generally the French could do little to resist Allied demands. While most of the French army was dissolved on Allied insistence, wave upon wave of Allied troops invaded France, until by September 1815 approximately 1,250,000 foreign soldiers were occupying sixty-one French departments, the cost of maintaining this huge army of occupation being borne by the local populations. The new peace settlement, the Second Treaty of Paris, imposed significantly harsher terms on France than its predecessor had done. France's frontiers were reduced essentially to those of 1789; 150,000 Allied troops occupied at French expense the northern and eastern departments until an indemnity of 700 million francs had been paid to the Allies; and works of art looted by the French during the Revolutionary and Napoleonic wars had to be returned to their former owners. Not surprisingly, therefore, the battle of Waterloo came to be regarded by Frenchmen as a national defeat. This reinforced the tendency, already common before 1815, to associate Napoleon and Bonapartism with nationalism and patriotism, and Louis XVIII and the Restoration Monarchy with defeat and humiliation at the hands of France's enemies.

Within France the political situation after Waterloo was more critical than it had been in the spring of 1814. In Marseilles, which like Bordeaux had suffered economically during the Revolutionary and Napoleonic wars and had generally become anti-Bonapartist, the news of Waterloo provoked on 24 June an explosion of popular violence in which fifty people were killed, 200 injured, and eighty houses or shops burnt down. Similar disturbances occurred at Toulon and throughout the towns of Provence. The violence tended to be spontaneous and random in character, though some of it was directed against prominent Jacobins and Napoleonic officials. In Avignon a mob even lynched a Napoleonic general and threw his body into the Rhône. Secret royalist societies in the area around Toulouse seized the opportunity provided by the administrative collapse at the end of the Hundred Days to unleash a 'white terror' against both supporters of Napoleon and moderate royalists. Protestants, whose religious rights had been recognized during the Revolution and the Empire and who had consequently tended to be pro-republican and pro-Bonapartist, became the victims of popular Catholic violence in Nîmes. Altogether there developed in several areas of provincial France a situation bordering on civil war, which in some instances lasted until November 1815. This intensified already-existing divisions and fears, associated the second Bourbon restoration with mob violence and Catholic and royalist extremism, and even to some extent challenged the authority of the government of Louis XVIII.

Since so many army officers and state officials had rallied to Napoleon or remained politically neutral during the Hundred Days, the government of Louis XVIII felt obliged to conduct a purge. The most famous victim, Marshal Ney, was tried by the Chamber of

Peers, found guilty, and executed on 7 December 1815. Labédoyère, the general who had handed Grenoble over to Napoleon, had been condemned and executed in August 1815, and three more generals were executed in 1816. Such executions were, however, the exception, partly because influential figures helped potential victims to escape. Sentences of exile were far more common with, in particular, all regicides and all members of the Bonapartist family being banished from France. Above all, state institutions and the royal administration were subjected to a political purge. Twenty-nine peers who had agreed to serve Napoleon during the Hundred Days were excluded from the Chamber of Peers, while the King created ninety-four new peerages. Within the prefectoral corps, thirty-eight prefects were dismissed and thirty-one transferred, and 115 sub-prefects dismissed and thirty-nine transferred. Altogether some 50,000 to 80,000 people, between a quarter and a third of all those in official posts, lost their jobs, from the Director of the Louvre to mayors of small rural communes. This purge was probably inevitable, given what had happened during the Hundred Days and the election in August 1815 of a Chamber of Deputies with a majority of extreme revenge-seeking royalists. However, the purge helped to undermine much of the work of reconciliation achieved during the first Bourbon restoration; the dismissals created bitterness and discontent amongst the tens of thousands of newly unemployed; and Louis XVIII's refusal to exercise his right of clemency, particularly in the case of Marshal Ney, 'the bravest of the brave', struck many of his subjects as cold-hearted vengeance.

In France the events of the years 1814–15, like the Revolutionary and Napoleonic eras generally, became the stuff of politics and legend. Frenchmen found it difficult not to take pride in Napoleon's many achievements, not to admire the Napoleonic domination of Continental Europe, and not to excuse Napoleon for his military defeats (by, for example, blaming 'General Winter' for the disaster in Russia of 1812 and Grouchy for the Allied victory at Waterloo). Napoleon himself, banished by the Allies to the remote island of St Helena in the South Atlantic, could successfully pose as a martyr and as a victim of the British, whose cruelty allegedly caused his early death (5 May 1821). The Treaties of 1815, as the final peace settlement came to be known, attracted resentment for many reasons: the constitutional monarchy of Louis XVIII tended to be viewed as British in inspiration and therefore as un-French; the surrender of Belgium, territories on the left bank of the Rhine, Savoy and Nice, were seen as an unacceptable loss of national territory; equally unacceptable were the gains made by the victors in 1815, particularly the dismemberment of Poland by Russia, Prussia and Austria, and the Austrian acquisition of the provinces of Lombardy and Venetia in northern Italy. Consequently, the Napoleonic legend lived on, as a reminder of past glories and inspiration for future greatness, while enthusiasm for the

Bourbons remained limited to a minority of royalists and Catholics. The overthrow of the Treaties of 1815 emerged as a new national goal, particularly the recovery of lost national territories and support for the suppressed peoples of Europe, especially the Poles and the Italians. Abroad, the national enemies of France tended to be identified as the monarchies and aristocracies of Prussia, Russia, Austria and Britain, while the French were misleadingly represented as the natural allies of the oppressed peoples of Europe in their struggles for liberation and national unification. Within France the political task remained to establish a widely accepted national identity.

During the years 1789 to 1815 few French families were unaffected by political events, and many Frenchmen were compelled, even if they did not choose, to make political choices and to take political sides. On the other hand, most of the French population lived in small towns or rural communities, were often illiterate and certainly did not read newspapers. For them the overriding preoccupation was economic survival, not politics. The population itself had risen from just over twenty-six million in 1789 to approximately thirty million in 1815. Paris had a population in 1815 of over 600,000, followed by Marseilles and Lyons with just over 100,000 and by Bordeaux and Rouen with just under 100,000. A further twelve French provincial cities had populations of 30,000 or more. Altogether in 1815 only some one and a half million of France's population lived in urban centres of more than 30,000 inhabitants. Probably about three-quarters of the active male labour force was engaged in agriculture, though some industries, notably textiles, were to be found in rural areas, and a considerable number of seasonal workers migrated annually from rural areas to urban centres. Nearly half the cultivated land of France was probably in peasant ownership by 1815, but the typical peasant landholding was barely adequate to support a family. The extensiveness of small-scale peasant agriculture, together with poor communications and an almost total absence of banks, encouraged low agricultural production and subsistence farming. Technological backwardness characterized most industrial production, which continued to be carried out by artisans in small workshops with fewer than five employees. This overwhelmingly rural and agricultural society was dominated by large land-owners, who constituted the bulk of the French élite. Thus, while politically and administratively France had changed enormously since 1789, economically and socially the changes were less obvious. The abolition of the seigneurial system in the countryside and of the trade guilds in the towns had removed burdens and restrictions from peasants and craftsmen; the property of the Roman Catholic Church and of some aristocrats and political suspects had been redistributed to existing property-owners and to peasants; and the economic blockades and the demands of war had distorted trading patterns and economic production, to the disadvantage of ports such as Bordeaux and Marseilles but to the temporary benefit of inland entrepôts and manufacturing towns such as Strasbourg and Mulhouse. Nevertheless, economically and socially France in 1815 remained a traditional society subject to traditional crises – economic crises caused by harvest failures and political crises caused by opposition within the élite to the Crown.

2 The Revolution of July 1830

There was nothing inevitable about the French Revolution of July 1830. The constitutional monarchy established in France in 1814, and re-established after Napoleon's Hundred Days in 1815, conformed to the constitutional norm for the states of Western Europe in the first half of the nineteenth century, represented a reasonable synthesis of France's Bourbon and Bonapartist past, permitted the small élite which dominated all aspects of French life to play a considerable role in local and national affairs, and promised peace at home and abroad, in welcome contrast to the domestic upheavals and foreign wars of the preceding twenty-six years. Admittedly, the institutions and ideology of the Bourbon monarchy had suffered devastating blows between 1789 and 1815. On the other hand, the legacy of centuries of tradition could still contribute to the popular acceptance and constitutional legitimacy of a Bourbon king in France; and France's Revolutionary and Napoleonic inheritance was by no means entirely negative for the restored Bourbons. The Roman Catholic Church and the aristocracy, which had so often opposed the Crown before 1789, had generally discovered a new identity of interest, and a new devotion to the monarchy, during their years of shared adversity. The creation in France of legal and institutional structures which were uniform and efficient meant that the kingdom was far easier to rule and administer than it had ever been before 1789. Finally, Napoleon had destroyed French republicanism as a significant political force, and the Hundred Day episode had brought Napoleon's meteoric career to an end and removed the prospect of any Bonapartist revival for the foreseeable future.

The Restoration Monarchy was ultimately overthrown by revolution principally because of its alienation of a majority of the politically active members of the French élite. The political élite of Restoration France can be defined quite precisely. The number of those entitled to vote in parliamentary elections (all of whom were adult Frenchmen and who paid annually 300 francs in direct taxes) rose from about 72,000 in 1814 to approximately 100,000 in 1830. Altogether, about one person in 360 out of France's total population was registered on the electoral roll (some of those who met the voting qualifications did not register out of laziness or a disinclination to become liable for jury service). The geographic distribution of voters inevitably reflected the geographic distribution of wealth and population, with some 10,000 to 12,000 qualifying to vote in the department of the Seine compared to only about forty in Corsica. The number of those eligible to stand for election as a deputy (Frenchmen aged forty or over who paid annually 1,000 francs in direct taxes) remained in the region of 15,000 for the whole of France. Again there were significant variations between departments, several of which had less than twenty potential deputies. Since not all those eligible to stand for election as deputies wanted to be actively involved in politics or were prepared to visit Paris for several months every year (deputies received no salary), the pool of prospective deputies was very small.

Members of the French élite had obvious common interests in supporting conservative economic and social policies and in maintaining a constitutional system which restricted participation in parliamentary politics to themselves. However, historically the élite was divided between those whose families belonged to the pre-1789 aristocracy or nobility and those whose families had prospered since 1789. This division encouraged very different historical attitudes and political loyalties. Royalists, generally those whose families belonged to the pre-1789 aristocracy or nobility, tended to be defenders of monarchical authority and of the Roman Catholic Church, while liberals, whose families had often prospered since 1789, tended to be defenders of traditional liberal freedoms and of the constitutional rights established in the Charters of 1814 and 1815. Royalists and liberals might clash over many issues, particularly those involving foreign policy, newspaper censorship, the powers and status of the Roman Catholic Church, and the constitutional rights of parliament and of the Crown.

The division within the French élite between royalists and liberals found expression not only in parliamentary politics but also in the Paris newspaper press. There were several royalist newspapers, of which the most important was *Le Journal des Débats*, the principal liberal newspaper being *Le Constitutionnel*. Since organized political parties did not exist in France at this time, since parliament was not in session for much of the year, and since journalists and newspaper editors fully exploited the first prolonged period of relative press freedom that France had ever enjoyed, newspapers could play a very important role by providing a forum for political debate and a focus for political leadership. Many of the leading political figures of the time regularly contributed to newspapers; and, while high costs and low circulations restricted the influence of newspapers, they did promote political interest and awareness among many of the disenfranchised, particularly in Paris and provincial towns where cafés and public reading rooms often maintained newspaper subscriptions.

From the end of the Hundred Days until the beginning of 1820 the Restoration Monarchy coped reasonably successfully with the many problems confronting France, despite labouring under a number of political handicaps. While the King himself, Louis XVIII, displayed considerable political moderation and astuteness, generally supporting sensible policies and appointing able ministers (such as Richelieu, Lainé and Decazes), his intelligence and reasonableness were not shared by his brother the Count of Artois or by his niece the Duchess of Angoulême, and he always had a potential rival in his cousin the Duke of Orleans. In the Chamber of Deputies ultra-royalists could be mindlessly provocative, notably in the first parliament after the Hundred Days, in which demands were made for the death penalty for those convicted of possessing the tricolour flag and for draconian measures against all those suspected of collaboration with Napoleon. At the other end of the political spectrum parliamentary criticism could come from liberals, especially after the elections of October 1818 when prominent liberals such as Lafayette, Manuel and Benjamin Constant became deputies. Outside parliament some ultra-royalists might be tempted to indulge in irresponsible plots and intrigues, while unrepentant Bonapartists might scheme to dispose of the Bourbons by assassination attempts or military *coups d'état*.

The most immediate and pressing problems facing the Restoration Monarchy after the Hundred Days were the payment of the indemnities owed to the victorious Allies and the ending of the occupation of French territory by foreign troops. With the help of loans from London and Amsterdam banking houses the indemnities had been paid off by the end of 1818, resulting in the withdrawal of all foreign troops from France two years ahead of schedule. This considerable achievement was gained at some social cost, particularly after the bad cereal harvests of 1816 and 1817, but it was of enormous symbolic value, saved the government the expense of paying for the foreign occupation, and allowed France to join the other European great powers as an equal at the diplomatic congress or conference of Aix-la-Chapelle (September–November 1818). The withdrawal of foreign troops from France greatly increased the importance of the French army, much of which had so strikingly demonstrated its disloyalty to the Bourbons and its attachment to Napoleon during the Hundred Days. A new army was created under the direction of Marshal Gouvion-Saint-Cyr, who, by a law of March 1818, introduced a much fairer system of military recruitment and restricted officer commissions to those who had risen through the ranks or who had graduated from military schools, which admitted cadets solely by competitive examinations.

The period from the end of the Hundred Days until the beginning of 1820 shows that the Restoration Monarchy could cope reasonably well with a range of difficult problems and could provide France with a reasonably satisfactory political system. However, at the beginning of 1820 a new period began, characterized by government-inspired reaction, a period which finally culminated in the Revolution of July 1830. On 13 February 1820 the assassination occurred of the Duke of Berry, who, since Louis XVIII, the Count of Artois and the Duke of Angoulême (the elder son of the Count of Artois) were all childless, was the heir presumptive to the French throne. The assassination was an isolated act by a deranged individual called Louvel, but it provoked an hysterical outburst of anti-liberalism from the ultra-royalists, who claimed that the liberalism of the government headed by Decazes had created a climate of opinion favourable to such acts of terrorism. Louis XVIII felt obliged to bow to this ultra-royalist pressure: he dismissed Decazes and invited Richelieu to form a new government; and a series of measures were introduced which allowed political suspects to be detained without trial for three months, re-established the censorship of newspapers, and gave a double vote in parliamentary elections to about 23,000 of the wealthiest voters. The liberal opposition in Parliament, and demonstrators in the streets of Paris, vigorously opposed these measures, but most members of the wealthy élite were prepared to accept some erosion of civil liberties in order to secure public order and political stability. Consequently, the measures were approved by large majorities in parliament; and liberal opposition candidates did not perform well in the parliamentary elections of November 1820 and of October 1821.

Hysterical anti-liberalism remained a potent force for some time after the assassination of the Duke of Berry, while the birth in September 1820 of a posthumous son to the Duke encouraged a wave of fervent royalism. In other respects, too, the political situation was favourable to reaction: in the Chamber of Deputies conservatives and ultra-royalists were in a strong majority; and the ageing King was becoming increasingly bored by politics, and increasingly under the influence of Madame du Cayla, who promoted the interests of the devout or clerical faction at Court. In these circumstances the Roman Catholic Church began to receive special protection and favour from legislation and government policies. A number of measures greatly strengthened the control of the Church over the state educational system. An ordinance of February 1821 placed secondary school teaching under the supervision of the Catholic bishops: in June 1822 the post of Grand Master of the University, or government minister for education, was re-established and given to a Catholic bishop; only Catholic bishops could licence primary school teachers after April 1824; and the dominant role of the Roman Catholic Church in French education received bureaucratic expression in August 1824 with the creation of a Ministry of Ecclesiastical Affairs and Public Instruction. Meanwhile during 1822 outrage against the Roman Catholic religion had been made a press offence, the Pantheon in Paris had been returned to the Roman Catholic Church after the removal of the remains of Voltaire and Rousseau, and nineteen bishops and archbishops had been created ecclesiastical peers and given seats in the Chamber of Peers. Since for historical

19

reasons the Roman Catholic Church in France had come to be regarded as a supporter of the Old Régime monarchy and of counter-revolution, these measures meant that the Church once again became a politically controversial institution, under attack from liberals, from opponents of the Bourbons, and from the discontented generally. Liberal journalists led anti-clerical crusades in the newspapers, suggesting that secret Catholic societies determined government policies, that priests engaged in all sorts of scandalous activities, and that the Jesuits, acting as agents of the Pope, were everywhere undermining French national interests. At the same time acts of vandalism desecrated church buildings, and Paris and other cities witnessed anti-clerical demonstrations.

After several years of ill-health, Louis XVIII died in September 1824. The last years of his reign had seen a new polarization in French politics between royalists and liberals, with the Crown and the Roman Catholic Church firmly identified with the royalists, though the situation was still far from critical. In foreign affairs the régime had scored a considerable success in the face of some vociferous but ill-supported liberal opposition. A French army had intervened in Spain in 1823 and, after fighting only one engagement of any significance (the capture of the Trocadero fortress), had restored the Bourbon King Ferdinand VII to the Spanish throne. This operation demonstrated that Louis XVIII had a reliable army, that France was once again a power to be reckoned with on the European continent, and that the goals of French foreign policy were no longer the spread of revolution or territorial conquest but instead the support of monarchical conservatism. Meanwhile at home the nation's finances had benefited from the prudent management of Villèle, and a series of good harvests had contributed to a revival of economic prosperity for which the régime, rightly or wrongly, could take the credit. Although Louis XVIII had antagonized liberals by approving reactionary government policies towards press censorship, education and the Roman Catholic Church, the prime responsibility for provoking the Revolution of July 1830 must lie with his successor, his brother the Count of Artois, who reigned as King Charles X.

Charles X differed from his brother Louis XVIII in many respects. Elegant in appearance and physically active for his age (sixty-seven in 1824), he had become, following a dissolute youth and after the death of his mistress in 1805, a devout Catholic and moral puritan whose chief amusements were hunting and card-playing. Before the outbreak of the Revolution of 1789 he had been an active supporter of absolute monarchy. Fleeing France after the storming of the Bastille he had become one of the first émigrés and one of the most prominent figures in the Counter-Revolution, joining the Duke of Brunswick's Austro-Prussian army which invaded France in 1792 and a British expedition which attempted to land on the French coast in 1795. His years of exile and counter-revolutionary activity had reinforced his belief in Catholicism and royal authority, so that throughout Louis XVIII's reign he had remained at the centre of ultra-royalism. On his accession Charles X tried to disarm his critics by abolishing press censorship, by retaining the existing government headed by Villèle, and by declaring his inviolable attachment to the Charter. Howevever, it was not long before the hopes of the ultra-royalists and the fears of the liberals began to be confirmed.

In 1825 Charles X boldly unfurled the banner of the Counter-Revolution. A new government-inspired sacrilege law, passed by parliament on 20 April, made the theft or vandalism of sacred objects used in Catholic worship punishable, in certain circumstances, by the death penalty. Although never invoked in practice, this draconian law demonstrated the extremes to which Charles X would go to protect the Catholic Church, and his intolerant and repressive attitude towards what might be interpreted as acts of opposition. Seven days later parliament approved another law which allocated nearly 1,000 million francs to compensate those whose property had been confiscated during the Revolution. About 25,000 claimants benefited, especially a handful of court aristocrats, chief of whom, ironically, was the Duke of Orleans. While projected before the death of Louis XVIII, the milliard of the émigrés, as it came to be known, had received a new impetus from Charles X. The total amount of compensation eventually paid (about 630 million francs) fell far short of the original target, the whole scheme could be defended on the grounds of equity, and all owners of nationalized property could now feel more secure. On the other hand, the scheme inevitably seemed divisive and provocative since it served to reopen old wounds, to split the élite into potential beneficiaries and potential contributors, and to give the general impression that Charles X wanted to undo the work of the Revolution. This impression was strengthened by Charles X having himself crowned on 29 May in Rheims cathedral, the traditional setting for French royal coronations. No king had been crowned in France since 1775, and the elaborate and antiquated ceremonies, which included Charles X prostrating himself before the Archbishop of Rheims and touching the scrofulous in order to heal them, struck many as at best constituting an expensive irrelevance and at worst portending a sinister revival of royal authority and clerical influence.

Opposition to these policies took a variety of forms. Constant criticism of the government came not only from the leading Paris liberal newspapers, *Le Constitutionnel* and *Le Courrier français*, but also from the most important conservative Paris newspaper, *Le Journal des Débats*. In June 1824 Chateaubriand, one of the most distinguished literary and political figures of his age, had been dismissed from his post as Minister of Foreign Affairs in the Villèle government, and thereafter in the pages of *Le Journal des Débats* had become one of Villèle's most persistent critics. In cruder terms, other newspapers, as well as pamphlets and political songs, denounced and ridiculed the government and the régime itself. The opposition fully exploited the opportunity for holding popular demonstrations provided by the funerals of public figures who had been critical of the régime, such as General Foy. Having served with distinction in the armies of the Revolution and the Empire, General Foy had rallied to Napoleon during the Hundred Days and had subsequently become a liberal member of the Chamber of Deputies, in which he had contested the milliard indemnity. His funeral in December 1825 attracted thousands of Parisians, and *Le Constitutionnel* helped to publicize a public subscription to raise funds for a statue of him. Already a common opposition front to Charles X was emerging, consisting of members of the liberal élite and of ordinary Parisians.

Despite such opposition Charles X and Villèle persevered with their counter-revolutionary policies. To help preserve the aristocratic land-owning class through encouraging the survival of landed estates, the government introduced a bill which would have enabled wealthy testators to leave most of their property to their eldest son and to have their estates entailed. Since primogeniture had been a principle of the Old Régime, and the equal division of inheritance a principle of the Revolution, the bill was widely regarded as being counter-revolutionary. In April 1826 both the Chamber of Peers and the Chamber of Deputies rejected the bill, an almost unprecedented government defeat which Parisians jubilantly celebrated. The pro-Catholic stance of the régime continued during 1826 with numerous government-supported ceremonies commemorating a papal jubilee, ceremonies which climaxed on 3 May when Charles X and the Archbishop of Paris participated in a service of expiation for Louis XVI's execution held in the largest square in Paris, the Place Louis XV. Formerly (1795–1815) and subsequently (since 1830) the Place de la Concorde, this square had been the site of the guillotine at the time of Louis XVI's execution, in memory of which the square officially bore the name of Place Louis XVI between 1826 and 1830. Meanwhile press attacks against the government and the régime continued with renewed vehemence; and public demonstrations accompanied the funerals in March 1827 of the Duke of La Rochefoucauld-Liancourt (a member of Napoleon's Chamber of Representatives during the Hundred Days and a liberal peer who had not voted for the condemnation of Marshal Ney and who had championed a variety of progressive causes) and in August 1827 of Jacques-Antoine Manuel (an opponent in August 1815 of the restoration of Louis XVIII and a vigorous parliamentary critic of Bourbon policies, particularly the invasion of Spain in 1823).

When confronted by criticism and opposition Charles X and Villèle resorted to repression and acts of questionable constitutional legality. At the end of December 1826 the government introduced a bill which would have imposed new restrictions on newspapers and other publications of a political character. After a stormy passage through the Chamber of Deputies, the bill had to be withdrawn on 17 April 1827 following rejection by the Chamber of Peers. Again the government had suffered an important parliamentary defeat, again opposition in the newspaper press had reached fever-pitch, and again a government setback had prompted jubilant celebrations in Paris. On 28 April Charles X reviewed the 20,000-strong Paris National Guard, the first such review since his accession. A minority of Guardsmen indicated their political and religious views by shouting slogans for the freedom of the press and the constitution and against the Jesuits. Over-reacting to what he regarded as indiscipline and responding to pressure from a clique of ministers and courtiers, Charles X dissolved the Paris National Guard the following day, thereby depriving his régime of the Guard's potential support for the maintenance of order in the capital and alienating this large body of former Guardsmen, who had all received military training and who were not disarmed. Two days after the end of the parliamentary session, a royal ordinance of 24 June reimposed press censorship. To forestall parliamentary criticism of a reactionary measure of doubtful constitutional legality, Charles X and Villèle decided to change the composition of parliament: on 6 November seventy-six new peers were created and new elections ordered for the Chamber of Deputies.

Charles X and his ministers hoped that successful French intervention in the Greek war of independence against the Turks, particularly French participation in the naval battle of Navarino (20 October 1827), would benefit government-supported candidates. However, the opposition was better organized than previously for the elections, which took place on 17 and 24 November. Political parties in the modern sense did not exist, but two organizations had been established to promote the election of liberal candidates, the oddly-named society Aide-toi, le ciel t'aidera (Help Yourself, and Heaven Will Help You) and Chateaubriand's Société des amis de la liberté de la presse (Society of the Friends of the Freedom of the Press). Helped by the unpopularity of the government's reactionary policies and by widespread concern arising from an economic recession, liberal candidates won some 180 seats. This huge increase in liberal representation in the Chamber of Deputies meant that in alliance with conservative opponents of Villèle they could out-vote the government. Villèle consequently resigned, being succeeded on 5 January 1828 by the more moderate Martignac. However, the economic crisis continued and the underlying political crisis remained – Charles X had lost majority support in the Chamber of Deputies.

In responding to the election results by accepting the resignation of Villèle and by appointing a more moderate ministry under Martignac, Charles X was acting as a constitutional monarch. He also gave his assent to a series of liberal measures: the suppression of the post of Director General of the Police; the ending of François

23

Guizot's suspension as Professor at the Sorbonne; the restricting of the influence of the Catholic clergy in primary school education (ordinance of 21 April 1828); the expulsion of Jesuits from teaching posts and the imposition of new controls on Catholic schools (ordinances of 16 June); the introduction of procedures making it more difficult for prefects and other officials to influence elections (law of 2 July); and the removal of some of the restrictions which had previously been imposed on the newspaper press (law of 18 July). All this almost amounted to a change of direction for the régime; and Charles X suddenly became quite popular, as was demonstrated during his tour of Alsace in August and September 1828. However, government repression of opposition continued with, for example, the prosecutions and convictions of Pierre Jean de Béranger, a composer of popular songs mocking the Bourbons, and Auguste Barthélemy, a satirist and writer of pro-Bonapartist poetry. Their widely reported trials and convictions (December 1828 and February 1829, respectively) transformed them into political martyrs. More important, Charles X was biding his time, waiting for a suitable moment in which to appoint a ministry more to his liking. On 8 April 1829 the government abandoned bills which would have made more local official posts elective after the bills had been defeated in the Chamber of Deputies by both liberals (who wanted more radical reforms) and ultra-royalists (who opposed any diminution of monarchical power). Charles X had refused to accept any amendments to make the bills acceptable to a majority of deputies, thereby almost certainly deliberately engineering an important government parliamentary defeat so as to give him an excuse to dismiss the Martignac ministry.

From the beginning of 1829 Charles X had been secretly planning to appoint a reactionary government. After waiting until the parliamentary session had ended and he had formed a suitable team, on 8 August he dismissed the Martignac ministry and announced new government appointments, the most important of which were the Prince of Polignac as Minister of Foreign Affairs, the Count of La Bourdonnaye as Minister of the Interior and the Count of Bourmont as Minister of War. The son of a favourite of Queen Marie Antoinette, Polignac had emigrated with his parents at the outbreak of the Revolution, had been imprisoned for nine years for alleged involvement in Cadoudal's plot to assassinate Napoleon, and had become after the Restoration a prominent member of the ultra-royalist faction surrounding Charles X, then Count of Artois. His acceptance from the Pope of the title of Prince (1820), and his marriage to an Englishwoman and comparatively long tenure of the French embassy in London (1823–9), suggested to the public that he was an ardent Catholic and anglophile. As a member of the Chamber of Deputies since 1815, La Bourdonnaye had given countless proofs of his intransigent ultra-royalism, notably in demanding ferocious punishments for those who had collaborated with Napoleon during the Hundred Days. Bourmont had joined the émigré Army of the Princes at Coblenz in 1791 and had subsequently served in the émigré army of the Prince of Condé and as a commander of royalist forces in the counter-revolutionary revolt in the Vendée. Eventually he had rallied to Napoleon, only to desert the Emperor four days before the battle of Waterloo and to produce damning testimony against Ney at the Marshal's trial. Thus in their different ways each of these new ministers virtually personified the Counter-Revolution.

The opposition press had a field day attacking such symbols of reaction. On 10 August 1829 Le Journal des Débats summed up its characterization of the Polignac ministry by the politically emotive words, 'Coblenz, Waterloo, 1815'. Other newspapers saw the appointment of the allegedly anglophile Polignac and Bourmont as part of a perfidious British plot and indulged in wild speculations and predictions – that the Polignac ministry would rebuild the Bastille, restore the privileges enjoyed by the aristocracy and the Catholic Church before 1789, and overthrow the constitution by a military coup d'état. In fact the Polignac ministry remained largely inactive in domestic affairs for months, apart from initiating legal proceedings against offending newspapers. Such proceedings served simply to stimulate the opposition. The 'Aide-toi, le ciel t'aidera' society formed or re-formed committees which helped liberals with parliamentary by-elections; tax boycotts were planned in Paris and in some provincial departments; Paris students established in January 1830 a left-wing society with its own newspaper, Jeune France; and new anti-government newspapers were founded (Le Temps in October 1829, Le National in January 1830), revived (Le Journal de Paris, La Tribune des Départements) or published more frequently (Le Globe, previously a weekly, became a daily in February 1830). Since 1815 never had the liberal and left-wing opposition been better organized, never had the political situation been less favourable to reaction.

On 2 March 1830 parliament reassembled to hear the Speech from the Throne, in which Charles X threatened to find the force necessary to surmount obstacles placed in his path by the opposition. In reply on 17 March the Chamber of Deputies approved by 221 votes to 181 an address implicitly asserting the responsibility of ministers to parliament and the necessity for any government to have majority support in parliament. In other words, the issue had ceased to be the unpopularity of government ministers and of government policies and had become the principle of the sovereignty of parliament, to which a majority of the representatives of the élite were firmly committed. In asserting the sovereignty of parliament, the 221 deputies and their supporters saw themselves as defenders of the constitution, not as radicals and still less as revolutionaries. For his part, Charles X interpreted this commitment to parliamentary sovereignty as opposition to the monarchical system; and he maintained that sovereignty ultimately lay with the Crown since Article 14 of the Charter allowed the monarch without the consent of parliament to issue regulations and ordinances deemed necessary for the execution of existing legislation and for the security of the state. After some delay Charles X and his ministers challenged their opponents by deciding on 16 May to dissolve parliament and to hold new elections on 23 June and 3 July. Three days later new Ministers of Justice and of the Interior were appointed, the new ministers being more willing than their predecessors to support Charles X if he invoked Article 14 of the Charter.

All shades of the opposition united to secure the re-election of the 221 deputies who had voted for the address in reply to the Speech from the Throne. Royalist newspapers, the administration, the bishops and even the King himself tried to exert influence on behalf of pro-government candidates, who nevertheless fared even worse than in previous elections. Of the 221 deputies who had voted for the address, 202 were re-elected, while the total number of opposition deputies rose to 274, compared to just 143 government supporters. Charles X and his ministers had hoped to exploit the success of French military operations in Algeria. In response to the depredations of Barbary pirates and the provocative behaviour of the Dey of Algiers towards the French, in January 1830 the Polignac ministry had decided to send a punitive expedition to Algeria. Eventually at the end of May a fleet of over 100 warships and nearly 500 merchant vessels transporting nearly 40,000 troops had set sail. The force successfully disembarked on the coast near Algiers, routed a numerically superior Algerian army on 19 June, and captured Algiers itself on 5 July. Charles X and Polignac exulted in what they regarded as a brilliant triumph: the capture of Algiers had been achieved at little cost (fewer than 500 French dead and the financial outlay could be offset by the captured treasure of the Dey of Algiers); it had demonstrated once again French military prowess and France's status as one of the great powers of Europe; it had delivered a satisfying snub to the British, whose government and diplomats had vigorously opposed the operation, and it could be presented as a Catholic crusade against Islam and as evidence of Divine support and favour for Charles X. However, opponents of the Polignac ministry had criticized the Algerian expedition as being expensive, dangerous and unnecessary, and as constituting an abuse of royal power; and in the parliamentary elections, partly perhaps because the news of the French victories arrived too late, the Algerian expedition did not help ministerial candidates – in fact the Baron d'Haussez, Minister of the Navy and chief planner of the expedition, lost his seat. After weeks of discussion, Charles X and Polignac reacted to their electoral defeat by deciding to sign on 25 July and have published on 26 July four ordinances: these imposed strict government censorship on newspapers, journals and political pamphlets, dissolved the newly elected Chamber of Deputies, reduced the total number of deputies to 258, a fifth of whom were to be elected annually on a more restricted franchise, and ordered new elections for September. If successfully enforced, the four ordinances would have completely undermined the liberty of the press and restricted the parliamentary franchise to a tiny minority, composed almost exclusively of the wealthiest landowners of France. Consequently, France would virtually have ceased to have been a constitutional monarchy.

The four ordinances had been drawn up in the greatest secrecy so there had been no attempt to win over public opinion. This preoccupation with secrecy, and Charles X's sublime over-confidence, also meant that there had been no military preparations either. With the cream of the French army in Algeria, and with the deployment of troops in Normandy (to deal with an outbreak of arson attacks) and on the Belgian frontier (since a Belgian revolt against Dutch rule seemed imminent), barely 12,000 regular soldiers were stationed in the Paris area in July 1830. Thus the people of Paris were no more prepared for the four ordinances than the royal authorities were for the explosive reaction which the ordinances immediately provoked. During the afternoon of 26 July deputies, journalists and lawyers met in private houses in Paris and in the editorial offices of *Le National*, where Adolphe Thiers drafted a protest against tyranny. This protest was signed by forty-four journalists and published in *Le National* and three other opposition newspapers on 27 July, despite an edict by the Prefect of Police prohibiting the publication of any newspaper without prior authorization. Individual copies of the protest were also printed in large numbers and distributed in Paris streets and cafés. A group of employers joined the protest by agreeing on 26 July to close their shops and workshops the following day, thus enabling large numbers of workers to take to the streets. Workers' protests began on the evening of 26 July with printers, whose livelihoods the ordinances directly threatened, demonstrating near the Bourse (the Stock Exchange) and the Palais Royal (the Paris residence of the Duke of Orleans) and outside the Ministry of Finance. Throughout the following morning crowds of workers gathered in and around the Palais Royal and, encouraged by the condemnation of the four ordinances in opposition newspapers, began to throw stones at police and soldiers. This led to violent incidents in which several demonstrators were killed. Their corpses were placed on stretchers and paraded through the streets to the cries of 'Death to the Ministers!' and 'Death to Polignac!' The Prefect of Police tried to silence opposition by issuing warrants for the arrest of the forty-four journalists and by dismantling the printing presses of the four newspapers which had printed their protest. Undaunted, opposition deputies and journalists continued to hold meetings on 27 July although they envisaged only legal resistance. However, the initiative was seized by working-class Parisians, determined not just to oppose the four ordinances but to overthrow the régime of Charles X by violence.

Paris workers were not directly affected by the constitutional crisis, since they could not vote in parliamentary elections; an enormous social and economic gulf separated them from opposition deputies and journalists; and many of them could not read a newspaper, let alone afford to buy one regularly. There were nevertheless many reasons why so many Paris workers were prepared in July 1830 to risk their lives fighting the soldiers of Charles X. Paris, of course, possessed a revolutionary tradition, which was always likely to surface at times of political conflict and economic recession. Anti-clericalism and opposition to what were considered to be ultra-royalist policies had become popular causes among Paris workers during the 1820s; and Charles X and Polignac, generally thought to personify clerical and ultra-royalist reaction, were widely detested. In 1825 an economic depression had begun in France and was sustained by a succession of bad harvests and by the exceptionally severe winter of 1829–30. The situation in Paris became particularly volatile, since the city had a far larger concentration of the unemployed than anywhere else in France. Over a quarter of the capital's 750,000 inhabitants were receiving some form of public assistance by July 1830. This political and economic discontent uniquely benefited liberals. Republicanism had not yet recovered from its virtual extinction during the Napoleonic period, Bonapartists lacked any organization and an effective pretender following Napoleon's death in 1821, and socialism had barely emerged, leaving liberalism as the only significant opposition movement to Charles X. Thus since 1820 Paris workers had tended to look to middle-class liberals for political leadership in what was apparently a common struggle against clericalism and ultra-royalism. In resorting to violence, the older generation of Paris workers could often draw on military experience gained in the Revolutionary and Imperial armies, while others had served in the Paris National Guard before its disbandment in 1827. Also there had been quite serious popular disturbances in Paris in June 1820 and in November 1827 to keep alive the tradition of popular protest in the capital.

During what became known as the three glorious days of 27, 28 and 29 July 1830, Charles X lost control of his capital. Having been informed of the first popular protests against the four ordinances, on the morning of 27 July he appointed Marmont commander of all military forces in Paris. Although a competent soldier, Marmont was not an inspired choice: his defection to the Allies in April 1814 had indelibly stained his reputation, while he believed that he had been passed over as a potential commander of the Algerian expedition and that the policies of the Polignac ministry were misguided. More important, he lacked any preparation for his command, had no tactical plan to put into operation, and did not have adequate military

28

forces at his disposal. Marmont ordered his troops to occupy the main strategic points in the capital, which was successfully accomplished. Yet crowds continued to roam the streets, tearing down representations of the royal coat of arms, raiding gunsmiths for weapons, constructing innumerable barricades and everywhere attacking soldiers of the Paris garrison. During the night an uneasy calm descended, though demonstrators destroyed many of the street lights. Early in the morning of 28 July the crowds assembled again, more numerous and more threatening than before. Marmont issued orders for troop reinforcements from provincial garrisons while Charles X, at last aware of the seriousness of his position, signed an ordinance establishing martial law in Paris. These moves totally failed to stem the mounting tide of violence or to redress the situation in the government's favour. The demonstrators, even more formidable in numbers, confidence and weaponry, managed to occupy important public buildings such as the Hôtel de Ville and the Cathedral of Notre-Dame. Meanwhile the soldiers, cut off by street barricades from orders, ammunition and supplies of food and drink, were becoming increasingly ineffective and in some cases were beginning to desert. During the night of 28–9 July nearly every street in the city was barricaded, forcing Marmont to concentrate his troops in defensive positions around the Louvre and the Tuileries. Further troop desertions during the morning of 29 July, and an unauthorized withdrawal of Swiss Guards from the Louvre, rapidly resulted in the remnants of Marmont's forces having to retreat in disorder up to the Champs Elysées. By the afternoon of 29 July the whole of Paris was in the hands of the insurgents.

Throughout the July Days Charles X remained at the Palace of Saint-Cloud on the outskirts of Paris, where he was cut off from events in the capital and could not communicate easily with Polignac and his other ministeres. Misled and misinformed by Polignac, he at first completely underestimated the force of the storm which he had provoked and refused to allow events to intrude into his daily routine of religious worship, hunting and card-playing. On 28 July he ignored a parliamentary deputation representing the liberal opposition which wanted to negotiate a cease-fire in return for the revocation of the four ordinances and the dismissal of the Polignac ministry. Only after he had learnt that the Tuileries Palace had fallen did he consent to making these concessions on 29 July. However, he at first failed to sign a document announcing the concessions; and he had no printing press at his disposal, and so could not communicate with his subjects. In any case by 29 July it was too late. The authority of Charles X had been overthrown in Paris and the political initiative and political power were being seized by others.

The overthrow of the authority of Charles X in his capital after just three days' streetfighting surprised and alarmed members of the liberal opposition. To prevent popular violence going unchecked a group of parliamentary deputies agreed during 29 July to establish at the Hôtel de Ville a municipal commission (which styled itself a provisional government the next day) and to create the Paris National Guard under the command of Lafayette. When the news of Charles X's proposed concessions eventually reached the deputies at the Hôtel de Ville they did not respond. The same day two liberal journalists, Adolphe Thiers and François Mignet, met at the house of a banker called Jacques Laffitte, and there drafted a proclamation calling for the overthrow of Charles X and his succession by his cousin the Duke of Orleans. Many copies of this proclamation were printed and distributed throughout Paris. Thiers, Mignet and Laffitte had acted on their own initiative, without the consent of the Duke of Orleans or the support of other members of the opposition. However, members of the Orleans family and the Duke himself cautiously welcomed the proclamation; and on 30 July representatives of the Chamber of Peers and the Chamber of Deputies agreed to offer the Duke of Orleans the office of Lieutenant-General of the Kingdom.

On 30 July a document signed by Charles X annulling the four ordinances and announcing a new ministry was at last brought to Paris, but representatives of the Chamber of Peers and the Chamber of Deputies agreed almost unanimously that the Duke of Orleans should be invited to serve as Lieutenant-General of the Kingdom. In doing so they recognized that the people of Paris would not now accept Charles X and that unless the power vacuum were quickly filled there might be mob rule in Paris leading possibly to a republic. Having been persuaded to come to Paris, the Duke of Orleans during the morning of 31 July accepted the post of Lieutenant-General, promising at the same time to respect the Chamber and to recognize the tricolour as France's national flag. This acceptance was immediately embodied into a declaration, of which 10,000 copies were printed and distributed. After members of the Chamber of Deputies under the presidency of Laffitte had met to ratify the Duke's acceptance, a huge procession accompanied the Duke from the Palais Bourbon to the Hôtel de Ville, where Lafayette as commander of the National Guard presented the Duke to an enthusiastic crowd.

Charles X, unable to rely on the effectiveness or loyalty of his army and at the age of seventy-two lacking the stomach for a civil war, capitulated: on 1 August he agreed to the proclamation of the Duke of Orleans as Lieutenant-General of the Kingdom, and on 2 August he abdicated in favour of his grandson, the Duke of Bordeaux. The abdication was communicated by the Duke of Orleans to the Chamber of Deputies, which, as he hoped and expected, ignored it. Far from proclaiming the Duke of Bordeaux as Henry V, Orleans wanted Charles X and his family out of France. When persuasion failed, on 3 August Orleans and Lafayette encouraged a Paris mob to set out for Rambouillet, a royal palace between Paris and Chartres to which Charles X had withdrawn. As his former ministers scattered,

Charles X finally agreed to being escorted to Cherbourg, from which on 16 August he sailed with his entourage to spend the last six years of his life in exile.

With Charles X out of the way what became known as the July Monarchy could be established. On 3 August the Duke of Orleans opened the new session of parliament. Addressing a minority of peers and deputies (sixty-seven out of a total of 365 peers and 194 out of a total of 428 deputies), he offered his services as a defender of law and order, as a guardian of the constitution, and as a supporter of an immediate examination of the organization of the National Guard, the use of juries in trials involving newspapers, the reform of local government, and the interpretation of Article 14 of the Charter. Against a background of popular unrest in Paris and in provincial cities such as Bordeaux, Lyons and Nantes, the Chamber of Peers and the Chamber of Deputies met daily to debate the institution of a new monarchy and the drafting of a new constitution. The Chamber of Deputies on 7 August reached agreement on several crucial issues. In view of the alleged violation of the Charter inherent in the four ordinances, the resistance of the citizens of Paris during the July Days, and the departure of Charles X and his family from France, the throne was declared to be vacant. The Charter itself was to be revised so that Roman Catholicism would be recognized as the religion professed by the majority of Frenchmen rather than the religion of the state, press censorship would be formally disallowed, the monarch's authority to issue ordinances in the interests of state security would be annulled, parliament would be able to initiate legislation, the tax and age qualifications required of parliamentary voters and candidates would be revised, and the tricolour would be adopted as France's national flag. Finally, the Duke of Orleans would be invited to accept these reforms and, having sworn before parliament to observe the revised Charter, to assume the title of King of the French. These resolutions were approved by large majorities in both the Chamber of Deputies (219 to thirty-three) and the Chamber of Peers (eighty-nine to ten with fourteen abstentions), though over a third of the deputies and over two-thirds of the peers did not attend to vote. Unsurprisingly, the Duke of Orleans enthusiastically welcomed the resolutions; and in a civil ceremony at the Palais Bourbon on 9 August he was formally proclaimed Louis-Philippe, King of the French.

It is difficult not to conclude that the main responsibility for the Revolution of July 1830 in France rests with Charles X. Admittedly, the economic recession which began in about 1825 and which continued until about 1832, caused such severe social distress that outbreaks of popular violence during this period were probably inevitable. However, outbreaks of popular violence should have been controllable provided that they did not have a pronounced political character, that they did not enjoy middle-class or élite support, and that the army remained loyal to the régime and effectively deployed. Equally inevitable, doubtless, were liberal reforms affecting parliament, local government, education, censorship, the courts and the Roman Catholic Church. Although significant liberal reforms would have involved the surrender of some royal prerogatives (at least in the opinion of Charles X), yet they could have been successfully introduced with France remaining a constitutional monarchy ruled by the senior line of the Bourbon dynasty. Charles X, though, needlessly and provocatively alienated all social classes with his anachronistic coronation at Rheims, his extreme pro-Catholic policies, his milliard indemnity scheme for royalist émigrés, and his crude attempts to stifle press and parliamentary criticism. His appointment and his initial support of the Martignac ministry suggested that he could have been a successful constitutional monarch, but, obstinately determined to push through his own policies regardless of the consequences, he could not play the role of a non-partisan political arbiter and he could not accommodate himself to the British concept of a loyal opposition. The decision to form a reactionary ministry headed by Polignac was an act of political folly while the four ordinances virtually sealed his fate, though even as late as 28 July 1830 he might have survived if he had dismissed the Polignac ministry and withdrawn the four ordinances. Through sheer ineptitude and incompetence Charles X lost what a French historian has described as Europe's most glorious throne and most beautiful kingdom.[2]

3 The July Monarchy and the February Revolution

Any explanation of the February 1848 Revolution in France must include an interpretation of the Revolution of July 1830. Some Legitimists, who had supported the Restoration Monarchy, professed to believe that Charles X had been overthrown by a conspiracy of Protestants and Jews with the help of a generous supply of gold coin provided by the British government. A similar thesis had already been developed to explain the Revolution of 1789; and it was suggested that this new example of the perfidy of Albion had been prompted by a British desire to avenge the French conquest of Algiers.[3] More persuasively, the socialist republican Louis Blanc in his *History of Ten Years* (1830–40) explained the outbreak and outcome of the July Days in class terms. The four ordinances had dealt the French bourgeoisie a double blow, for the measures against parliament and the newspaper press had threatened their political power and their political influence. Therefore on 27 July 1830 the most politically active members of the bourgeoisie successfully incited the people of Paris to rise against the régime of Charles X, thus initiating a revolutionary movement. However, this popular revolutionary movement was betrayed and abandoned when the bourgeois political leadership engineered the accession of Louis-Philippe instead of proclaiming a republic. The establishment of the July Monarchy constituted a triumph for the bourgeoisie: the new king, the new government and the new constitution all reflected their interests; and after July 1830 artisans and workers were repressed within France, while abroad French governments refused to assist revolutionary and nationalist movements. Contemporaries as politically diverse as the liberal aristocrat Alexis de Tocqueville and the revolutionary communist Karl Marx shared this view of the July Revolution as a bourgeois triumph and of the July Monarchy as a bourgeois régime, though the ideas of Louis Blanc were modified and developed. For example, Karl Marx and Alfred Delvau (personal secretary to the left-wing republican Ledru-Rollin when Minister of the Interior in 1848) maintained that the chief victors of the July Days were a particular section of the bourgeoisie, the so-called financial aristocracy;

and it was also suggested that the 1830 Revolution should be seen in the context of France's revolutionary tradition, as a resumption of the great revolutionary effort interrupted by the overthrow of Robespierre in July 1794, and as a repetition of the tactical and temporary alliance of 1789 between the leaders of the bourgeoisie and the popular movement of Paris.[4]

Professor David Pinkney has identified 'the Orleanist solution to the crisis of July and August 1830' as having been 'the work of a handful of men', namely two bankers (Laffitte and Périer), two lawyers (Dupin and Bérard), one professor (Guizot), two writers and journalists (Constant and Thiers), and five aristocrats (Broglie, Lafayette, Sébastiani, Laborde and Delessert). In other words, those responsible for engineering the accession of Louis-Philippe belonged to three different social groups – the upper bourgeoisie, the professional middle class and the aristocracy. While in social terms they all belonged to the French élite, it was their opposition to Charles X and Polignac which united them, a political unity which proved fragile. Many of them moved into official posts after July 1830 but were soon disagreeing so fundamentally amongst themselves that Broglie and Guizot resigned from the government at the end of September and Lafayette from the command of the Paris National Guard at the end of December. Thus they should be seen, not so much as political leaders of the bourgeoisie, but rather as a temporary coalition of the opponents of Charles X and Polignac whose members belonged to different sections of the French élite, including the aristocracy.

The class analysis seems to be more applicable to the combatants against the régime of Charles X during the July Days. Professor Pinkney has established that, typically, they were male, aged between twenty and thirty-five, and artisans or skilled workers in traditional Parisian trades, with stonemasons, joiners, carpenters, cabinet-makers and locksmiths being particularly prominent.[5] Members of the same social group, the so-called *sans-culottes*, had predominated in the Paris popular movement between 1789 and 1795, which suggests that there are genuine parallels between the Revolution of 1830 and the Revolution of 1789; and, as in 1789, there are grounds for arguing that élite liberal political leaders betrayed and abandoned those who had actually fought and died in the revolutionary cause.

The new King, Louis-Philippe, was a Bourbon, but he belonged to the junior line of the Bourbon dynasty of France. Descended from Louis XIII (1601–43), he was a cousin of Charles X. Besides proximity to the French throne, Louis-Philippe derived from his Bourbon inheritance immense wealth and a tradition of political rivalry with the monarch. This rivalry had become an unbridgeable chasm as a result of his father's public opposition to the Crown before 1789, his suspected encouragement of the storming of the Bastille (14 July 1789), and, above all, his parliamentary vote in favour of the death penalty for Louis XVI (15 January 1793).Louis-Philippe himself as Duke of Orleans served as an officer in the French army after the overthrow of the constitutional monarchy; and, as a young man (he was born in October 1773), he distinguished himself at the battles of Valmy (20 September 1792) and Jemappes (6 November 1792), victories which permitted the newly established French Republic to occupy Belgium. However, Louis-Philippe became implicated with his commanding officer, General Dumouriez, in a plot to restore the constitutional monarchy, and with Dumouriez deserted to the Austrians in April 1793. This act of treason led to the arrest of his father, who was eventually tried and executed (6 November 1793). Meanwhile Louis-Philippe had begun a life of exile, which took him to Switzerland, Scandinavia, the United States, Malta, Sicily and England, and which ended only in May 1814 with the first Bourbon restoration. Initially relations between Louis-Philippe and Louis XVIII were quite friendly, but after the Hundred Days, during which Louis-Philippe on his own initiative disbanded the Royal Guard and sought refuge in England instead of following Louis XVIII to Belgium, the old animosities returned. Excluded from playing any significant official role by both Louis XVIII and Charles X, Louis-Philippe devoted his energies to his personal fortune and to his expanding family. Through shrewd management, various inheritances, and compensation payments from the milliard indemnity of 1825, the wealth of the Orleans family reached fabulous proportions; and by his wife (a Sicilian princess related to the Spanish Bourbons) between 1810 and 1824 he had ten children, eight of whom survived infancy.

In political terms Louis-Philippe is difficult to categorize. He was a Bourbon, a descendant of Louis XIII, and a king of France, but he was also the son of a regicide who had inherited and maintained a family tradition of hostile relations with the reigning monarch. Just as his father had espoused the Revolution by calling himself Philippe Egalité and by securing his election in Paris to the Convention parliament, but then, accused of plotting against the Revolution, had fallen victim to the Terror, so Louis-Philippe had fought in the armies of the Republic only to desert to the enemy and to join the emigration. By accepting the French throne in August 1830 Louis-Philippe confirmed the overthrow of Charles X, consolidated the Revolution, and undermined the monarchical principle of legitimacy, but simultaneously he scotched the possibility of a republic and, since no election or plebiscite was held, ignored the revolutionary principle of popular sovereignty. Louis-Philippe's title reflected the ambiguity of his position: recalling the precedents of Louis XVI in 1791 (proclaimed King of the French) and of Napoleon in 1804 (proclaimed Emperor of the French), he became King of the French rather than King of France and Navarre (as Louis XVIII and Charles X had been styled), thus suggesting a monarch of a people rather than a ruler of a kingdom. Similarly, while the tricolour was readopted as France's national flag, signifiying a continuity with France's Revolutionary and Napoleonic past, a rather bulbous crown became the official symbol of the régime, emphasizing its monarchical character.

Louis-Philippe's designation as a bourgeois king is misleading. Admittedly, his personal life-style could be considered bourgeois. An elaborate Court etiquette, and traditional Bourbon pastimes and pleasures such as hunting, royal mistresses and an ostentatious indulgence in religious devotions, held no attraction for him. Instead, until deterred by assassination attempts, he liked to walk around Paris streets carrying an umbrella; he sent his sons to be educated at an ordinary Parisian school (the Henri IV College); and he enjoyed reminiscing at length and relaxing in the comfortable circle of his numerous children and of his devoted wife and equally devoted sister, the Princess Adélaïde. Yet his enormous wealth alone disqualified him from bourgeois status. Nor was he the constitutional representative of the bourgeoisie or of a bourgeois ideology. Throughout his reign he never became subservient to any social class or to any political faction, being determined, as he put it in a remark recorded in de Tocqueville's memoirs, to drive his own cart. Altogether the July Monarchy and Orleanism stood for little more than constitutional monarchy and the monopoly of political power by the wealthier classes.

As in 1814 and 1815, the change of ruler and the change of régime were accompanied by numerous resignations and dismissals from official posts and to some extent by a change in the character of the élite. The members of the Polignac ministry, of course, all lost office, and Polignac and three of his former colleagues who had failed to escape into exile suffered imprisonment in the fortress of Vincennes. In October 1830 violent Parisian demonstrators demanded their executions but they were soon released. Those appointed to ministerial office during the reign of Louis-Philippe tended to belong to one of three broad categories: either they were aristocrats, such as Broglie, Molé, Montalivet, Salvandy and Soult; or they were wealthy members of the upper bourgeoisie, such as the bankers Laffitte and Périer; or they were what might be described as professional politicians, such as Duchâtel, Guizot, Thiers and Villemain. The aristocrats usually belonged to that section of the French aristocracy which had served Napoleon in some official capacity and which had joined the liberal opposition of the late 1820s. Their presence in high office gave the allegedly bourgeois régime of Louis-Philippe an aristocratic flavour, though the aristocratic domination of government of the Restoration period had ended, and the political significance of the French aristocracy became much less than that of their British counterparts. The examples of Laffitte and Périer notwithstanding, wealthy members of the bourgeoisie did not usually play a very active role in national politics, doubtless being anxious to concentrate on their business interests. Instead, there emerged a comparatively new breed of politician, intelligent, industrious and ambitious, often pursuing an additional career as a writer, journalist, academic or lawyer, and normally too independent-minded to be the mere spokesman of the bourgeoisie or indeed of anybody else.

An analysis of the official élite of the July Monarchy also reveals an aristocratic presence, though again the aristocracy was gradually becoming less important. Since Napoleon's concordat with the Vatican of 1801 members of the hierarchy of the Catholic Church had not lost their posts with a change of régime, although some Legitimists vainly expected episcopal resignations in 1830; and senior French churchmen tended to be remarkably long-lived. Consequently, as late as 1840 forty out of eighty bishops and archbishops came from noble families, and twenty-eight of them had emigrated during the Revolution. However, the July Monarchy distanced itself from the Catholic Church; bishops and archbishops ceased to be members of the Chamber of Peers after 1830; and, while nobles and aristocrats continued to receive episcopal appointments under the July Monarchy, they slowly ceased to dominate the ecclesiastical hierarchy. Many of those occupying senior government posts, on the other hand, either felt obliged to resign after July 1830 or were dismissed. Following the overthrow of Charles X a large number of Legitimist aristocrats resigned from government service and retired to their country estates, a phenomenon which became known as the emigration into the interior, while many office-holders who did not choose to resign fell victim to a series of drastic purges. Nevertheless, the social character of the new official élite was not so very different from the old. The senior ranks of the diplomatic service remained virtually a noble and aristocratic preserve; and the more important judges, administrators and civil servants overwhelmingly came from an upper-middle-class background, though usually they were not now nobles or aristocrats. In the officer corps of the army and navy Legitimist aristocrats were frequently replaced by Napoleonic veterans, while the military and naval colleges which trained future officers recruited predominantly from the sons of officers, government officials and land-owners.

The new constitution, known as the Charter of 1830, generally consolidated political power in the hands of the wealthy land-owning class, a significant proportion of whom were aristocrats or nobles. A law of 29 December 1831 abolished the hereditary peerage so that the Chamber of Peers became in effect composed of life peers. Nevertheless nearly a third of the membership of the Chamber of Peers belonged to the pre-1789 aristocracy or nobility, with a slightly higher proportion belonging to families ennobled by Napoleon. Considerably more than half the peers had served the state, including Napoleon's imperial régime, in some official capacity. Most peers were land-owners, and a generous sprinkling were engaged in a liberal profession or involved in business or commerce, so that typically they were men of wealth and distinction. However, many peers did not regularly attend the sessions at the Luxembourg Palace, either because of their advanced age or because of other commitments; and altogether the Chamber of Peers played a less important role in national politics than the Chamber of Deputies. According to a law of 19 April 1831 candidates for election to the Chamber of Deputies had to pay annually 500 francs rather than 1,000 francs in direct taxes and be aged at least thirty rather than forty. This obviously enlarged the pool of prospective parliamentary candidates, but the social composition of the Chamber of Deputies did not change very markedly. It has been calculated that the 459 deputies in 1840 included 175 office-holders, 137 land-owners, eighty-seven members of a liberal profession, and sixty bankers, manufacturers or merchants. The tax qualification for the parliamentary franchise was also lowered, from 300 to 200 francs, which in 1831 roughly doubled the size of the electorate at about 170,000, a figure which had risen to over 240,000 by 1846. The geographic distribution of those who met these tax qualifications was inevitably uneven, the highest concentrations being in the departments of the Seine (which included Paris), Nord, Pas-de-Calais and Calvados, and the lowest in the thinly populated mountainous departments of the Basses-Alpes and Hautes-Pyrénées. Many peers and deputies also exercised power at a local level in the general councils of each department. These general councils usually consisted of thirty members who, following a law of 22 June 1833, were elected in each canton by the fifty most important taxpayers. This meant that in poor cantons many could vote in local elections who could not vote in parliamentary elections; and, while land-owners predominated in the general councils, the presence of a city like Lyons or Marseilles within a department could result in representatives of the commercial bourgeoisie gaining power at a departmental level. An even wider franchise operated for the election of municipal councils according to a law of 21 March 1831, which enabled more than two million Frenchmen to vote in municipal elections. The powers of municipal councils were not large, and mayors, although they had to be elected councillors, were appointed by the King or (in communes with a population of less than 3,000) by the prefect. Nevertheless municipal councils were the most democratic institutions of July Monarchy France.

In economic terms France during the July Monarchy was still a traditional society, though a more modern capitalist economy was slowly developing. Agriculture remained overwhelmingly the major economic sector. Owners of agricultural estates dominated the élite; land-ownership was the most important form of investment, even for the Paris bourgeoisie; and agriculture provided a livelihood for approximately 60 per cent of the economically active population. Before the construction of railways many regions of France lacked good communications, so much agricultural production was necessarily restricted to meeting local demands for food. This discouraged agricultural specialization and improvement, as did the prevalence of small agricultural units farmed by peasant proprietors or tenants and the absence of adequate banking facilities. Poor communications and limited investment similarly restricted most manufacturing production, which typically took the form of artisan craft workshops rather than of factories. However, the foundations of a more modern economy were being laid. After 1830 public expenditure on roads and canals increased significantly, while the first railway line in France, from St Etienne to Lyons, was opened in 1832. Subsequently railway lines were constructed between Paris and the neighbouring towns of St Germain-en-Laye and Versailles, and in the provinces between Strasbourg, Mulhouse and Basle and between Nîmes, Montpellier and the Mediterranean port of Sète. From 1843 railway lines linked Paris to Orleans and Rouen; and by 1847 the Paris–Orleans line had been extended to Tours and the Paris–Rouen line to Le Havre, while a third railway line connected Paris, Amiens, Lille and Brussels. The beginnings of what amounted to a transport revolution were accompanied by the establishment of banks in nearly every town of any importance, the introduction of new technology in industries such as newspaper printing and textiles, and the expansion of metallurgy, textile manufacture and the consumption of coal. Mainly as a result of seasonal or more permanent migration from rural areas, many urban populations experienced rapid growth. Thus the population of Paris rose from 786,000 in 1831 to just over a million in 1846, that of Marseilles from 145,000 in 1831 to 183,000 in 1846, and that of Lyons from 134,000 in 1831 to 178,000 in 1846. Paris, the political, administrative and cultural capital, as well as France's most important industrial and commercial centre, was obviously exceptionally populous. However, in addition to Marseilles and Lyons, a number of provincial cities became thriving industrial and commercial centres during the July Monarchy, including Bordeaux, Le Havre, Rouen, Nantes and Strasbourg. There was also the relatively new phenomenon of a rapidly expanding town dominated by one or two industries, such as Elbeuf (wool), Le Creusot (metallurgy), Lille (cotton and linen), Limoges (paper and porcelain), Mulhouse (cotton), Roubaix (wool) and St Etienne (metallurgy and textiles). The land-owning élite was by no means an economically inactive rentier class, cut off from these developments: as investors and directors, wealthy land-owners frequently became involved in banks, insurance companies, railways, coal mines, iron foundries, sugar refineries and similar enterprises. However, they thereby inevitably helped to create a new world – industrial and commercial, urban and proletarian, capitalist and bourgeois.

The politics of July Monarchy France, while obviously reflecting the dominant position of the wealthy land-owning class, have been interpreted in different ways. It has been argued that the liberal coalition which successfully resisted Charles X and Polignac and secured the enthronement of Louis-Philippe subsequently fell apart through personal and political differences, and that the resultant rivalries and conflicts contributed to the revolutionary upheaval of February 1848. Also an ideological distinction has been drawn between the so-called Party of Movement, those who regarded 1830 as the beginning of an era of reform, and the so-called Party of Resistance, those who opposed any significant change to the 1830 settlement, and that it was the triumph of the latter over the former and the consequent immobilism which brought down Louis-Philippe. More starkly, the political history of Louis-Philippe's reign can be interpreted in terms of revolution and counter-revolution: the 1830 Revolution allegedly was not just confined to Paris, but extended into the provinces, and was not just confined to 1830, but continued until at least 1834 or 1835. Although the Counter-Revolution had apparently triumphed by the mid-1830s, the Revolutionary movement had in fact been defeated rather than destroyed, and towards the end of 1847 and beginning of 1848 it re-emerged to mount a successful challenge to the Orleanist régime. Finally, the politics of the July Monarchy can be interpreted simply in terms of survival: survival for governments, which often could not count on the support of a reliable majority in the Chamber of Deputies; and survival for the régime itself, threatened as it was by Legitimist risings, republican conspiracies, labour unrest, assassination attempts, Bonapartist *coups* and natural disasters.

The interpretation of the politics of the July Monarchy is complicated by a number of factors. The régime lacked any clear ideological foundation. Although born in revolution, the régime quickly became embarrassed by its revolutionary origins. Significantly, the famous painting by Delacroix representing the July Days, *Liberty Leading the People*, was withdrawn by the authorities from public exhibition in 1833. Liberalism and the *juste-milieu* scarcely amounted to a coherent ideology, and in any case Orleanist governments responded to the threats confronting them by adopting illiberal and repressive measures. Attempts were made to exploit Bonapartism and the Napoleonic legend: paintings depicting Napoleonic battle scenes went on display at the Palace of Versailles; the construction in Paris of the Arc de Triomphe, commemorating Napoleon's victories, was inaugurated in 1836; and in 1840 the remains of Napoleon were ceremonially transported from St Helena to Paris for reburial in the chapel of the Invalides. However, Louis-Philippe was too unmartial to be identified with Napoleon, while the July Monarchy was too materialistic and too lacking in glory to pose successfully as the heir to Napoleon's Empire. Some electors and deputies might at least profess a loyalty to Legitimism, Bonapartism, republicanism or even Orleanism, but clear ideological commitment was the exception rather than the rule, although consistent voting patterns can be discerned in the case of many deputies. At elections parliamentary candidates usually stood as either supporters or opponents of the government in power, and in the Chamber prominent deputies usually attracted a small band of followers, but organized political parties did not develop. For most politicians, personal ambitions and personal rivalries provided the motive for political behaviour, although genuine political differences could emerge, particularly over foreign policy. The uncertain political loyalties all this helped to create partly explain why there were fifteen different governments between July 1830 and October 1840, with only three governments lasting longer than a year and six lasting less than three months. Yet a considerable degree of ministerial continuity accompanied this government instability, since the King, to whom the Charter of 1830 had given the power to appoint and dismiss government ministers, tended to rely on a limited circle of peers and deputies.

The ministerial instability of the 1830s was also partly due to the succession of crises confronting French governments throughout that decade. Although Charles X had been overthrown, and the July Monarchy established, with remarkable speed and with remarkably little resistance, in the ten years following 1830 the very survival of the Orleanist régime must often have seemed in doubt. Legitimists did not rally to Charles X's defence, even during his slow progress into exile, but many of them ostentatiously displayed their political loyalties by resigning from public office and by participating in events such as the mass held in the Paris church of Saint-Germain-l'Auxerrois to commemorate the assassination of the Duke of Berry (13 February 1831). The gathering of a fashionable crowd for such a purpose at a church in central Paris provoked a violent riot, in which the church and the residence of the Archbishop of Paris were sacked. At the end of April the following year the Duke of Berry's widow landed near Marseilles and travelled secretly to the traditionally royalist region of the Vendée, south of Brittany, with the intention of leading a rising. The whole affair at once became a complete fiasco: the government had learnt of her plans; the prospect of armed revolt attracted neither aristocrats nor peasants; and the Duchess herself was eventually captured and found to be pregnant. Yet over 100 lives were lost in several clashes between royalist bands and government troops; and the Duchess, imprisoned in the fortress of Blaye, could pose as a martyr to the royalist cause. Despite this disaster Legitimism retained the loyalty of many aristocrats and some Catholics; and it lingered on in the Vendée and, to a lesser extent, in parts of southern France, particularly the regions around Toulouse, Avignon, Aix-en-Provence and Marseilles.

A more serious threat to the Orleanist régime seemed to be presented by popular protest. The economic recession which had begun in 1827 continued until at least 1832, so that after July 1830

41

economic factors often helped to fuel explosions of popular violence. Immediately following the July Days power vacuums developed in the provinces as prefects and other local officials resigned or were replaced, as provisional self-appointed committees attempted to take over the administration of towns and departments, and as army and National Guard units became unreliable. In towns workers went on strike, bakeries were ransacked and tax registers destroyed, while in rural areas châteaux were threatened, grain convoys hijacked and forest codes disregarded. The most serious popular disturbances occurred in Lyons during November 1831 when silk-workers protested violently against new wage rates. The demands accompanying such violence were invariably economic – for higher wages and a shorter working day, for the expulsion of foreign workers, for the destruction of machines, and for a reduction in the price of bread. However, particularly in view of the régime's concern with stability and order, economic protest often acquired a political character and involved confrontation with government forces. A new law was passed against unlawful assembly (10 April 1831); and the invariable government response to any major popular protest was to call in the army.

In 1832 a cholera epidemic reached France, hitting urban populations particularly hard, with over 18,000 victims in Paris alone. Also by 1832 government repression at home, and the abandonment of revolutionary and nationalist movements abroad, had encouraged popular alienation from the Orleanist regime and even the spread of republicanism, especially in Paris. One of the victims of the cholera epidemic was General Lamarque. After distinguished service in the armies of the Revolution and the Empire, he had rallied to Napoleon during the Hundred Days and had commanded the troops who suppressed the royalist rising against Napoleon in the Vendée. Exiled from France for over three years in July 1815, he had become a political opponent of the Restoration Monarchy and eventually in 1828 had been elected to the Chamber of Deputies, where he had joined the liberal opposition. While welcoming the July 1830 Revolution, he had subsequently delivered a series of impassioned parliamentary speeches urging the overthrow of the Treaties of 1815, particularly through the re-unification of Belgium to France and the re-establishment of Poland. Thus for Bonapartists, frustrated nationalists and opponents of the July Monarchy Lamarque could serve as a symbolic figure; and the elaborate official funeral on 19 May 1832 for Casimir Périer, head of a repressive government since 13 March 1831 and another victim of the cholera epidemic, could serve as both a provocation and an inspiration. Consequently Lamarque's funeral on 5 June 1832 was turned into a demonstration of political opposition to the government and the régime. Clashes with the police provoked a riot and the erection of street barricades. Order was quickly restored, though it took the next day and artillery to dislodge about 100 republicans who had barricaded themselves in and around a church near the Paris Hôtel de Ville. The violence did not attract much popular support; potential republican leaders such as Lafayette and Armand Carrel (editor of *Le National*) did not back the rioters; and police, soldiers and National Guardsmen were generally loyal and effective. Nevertheless a panicked government, blaming the disturbances on an improbable combination of royalist rebels and extreme republicans ('*les alliés des chouans et les admirateurs de Robespierre et de Marat*'[6]), placed Paris under martial law, closed the Ecole Polytechnique, and dissolved the artillery corps of the Paris National Guard.

Despite its association with futile political violence, through newspapers and through organizations such as the Society of the Rights of Man, republicanism gradually became more influential, particularly in Paris and in a few provincial cities. The government responded with a new law (10 April 1834) requiring all associations to obtain official authorization, thus enabling the government to control republican clubs and societies. The passage of this measure through parliament coincided with another workers' rising in Lyons. The situation in Lyons was always likely to be volatile, due to the exceptionally large concentration of workers there. After the revolt of November 1831, which had resulted in 275 deaths, a radical political culture began to flourish among the Lyons workers, of whom an untypically large proportion seem to have been literate; and the Lyons silk industry failed to share in the general recovery of the French economy after 1832. A strike by silk-workers over wage rates in February 1834 was followed by a further decline in the demand for silk, by the opening of the trial of the strike leaders, and by the new law on associations. All this triggered off a six-day confrontation between workers and soldiers with over 300 killed (9–14 April 1834). In Paris an inaccurate report that Lyons had fallen to the rebels, and the government's suspension of *La Tribune* (an important republican newspaper) and arrest of about 150 leading members of the Society of the Rights of Man, led on 13 and 14 April to twenty-four hours of violence and some twenty-five deaths, including innocent civilians killed by soldiers in the so-called massacre of the Rue Transnonain. Less-significant outbreaks of violence occurred at the same time in several provincial cities.

Although the suppression of the Lyons revolt and the Paris riots of April 1834 demonstrated the apparent futility of political violence, the régime continued to be threatened by violence. During a review of the Paris National Guard by Louis Philippe on 28 July 1835, the anniversary of the Revolution of 1830, an 'infernal machine' consisting of twenty-four muskets bound together discharged a murderous volley from an upper-storey window into the royal procession. The King escaped but eighteen were killed, including Marshal Mortier, the Minister of War, and a further twenty-three were seriously wounded. The perpetrators of this act of terrorism were a handful of republicans led by a Corsican adventurer called Joseph Fieschi, acting entirely on their own initiative; and news of the outrage provoked a wave of sympathy and support for the royal family. Yet Louis-Philippe and his government chose to blame the incident, at least partly, on irresponsible newspapers which frequently seemed only too willing to incite and condone political violence. Parliament was hastily recalled and in a near-panic atmosphere passed severe measures against the newspaper press. What became known as the September 1835 press laws were designed virtually to silence Legitimist and republican newspapers by extending the definition of criminal libel, by introducing jury judgements by a simple majority verdict, by increasing the financial penalties for press offences, and by controlling the publication of political caricatures. Some republican newspapers, such as *La Tribune*, had already been forced to cease publication because of official harassment, and approximately thirty more republican newspapers were closed down by the September 1835 press laws. However, the main Paris republican newspaper, *Le National*, continued to appear; and several important new left-wing newspapers and journals were successfully established, including *La Revue du progrès* (1839) by Louis Blanc, *Le Populaire* (1841) by Etienne Cabet, *La Revue indépendante* (1842) by Pierre Leroux and George Sand, *La Démocratie pacifique* (1843) by Victor Considérant, and *La Réforme* (1843) by Louis Blanc, Ferdinand Flocon and Ledru-Rollin. Moreover, the government's attempts to censor and silence the opposition newspaper press earned the hostility and contempt of many journalists and of much of the newspaper-reading public.

Legal restrictions on the newspaper press also failed to end political violence directed against the Orleanist régime. In October 1836 such violence took the unexpected form of an attempt by Louis Napoleon Bonaparte to subvert the military garrison of Strasbourg. The son of Louis Bonaparte, who reigned as King of Holland from 1806 to 1810, and the nephew and heir of the Emperor Napoleon, Louis Napoleon Bonaparte had been forced to leave France with his mother in 1815 and had subsequently lived in exile, chiefly in Switzerland. Hoping to exploit the considerable disaffection which existed towards the July Monarchy, and to capitalize on the magic name of Napoleon and on the appeal of the Napoleonic legend, on 30 October 1836 Louis Napoleon Bonaparte tried to rally the soldiers of the Strasbourg garrison to his cause. He succeeded with the 4th Artillery Regiment, Napoleon's old regiment, and with some other artillerymen and engineers, but the military governor of Strasbourg refused to support him, and he was arrested and imprisoned when he tried to win over an infantry regiment. Anxious to avoid the embarrassment of a political trial, Louis-Philippe and his government had Louis Napoleon Bonaparte transported to the United States. For the unsuccessful pretender the Strasbourg affair obviously constituted a pathetic and disastrous attempt to repeat his uncle's 'Flight of the Eagle' of April

44

1815. On the other hand, no lives had been lost; the French public had been reminded of his imperial claims and of the Bonapartist cause; and public celebrations in Strasbourg greeted the acquittal of his accomplices by a jury in January 1837.

Two further episodes demonstrated the apparent futility of political violence. In 1838 the Society of the Seasons, consisting of a small group of anarchist republicans, was founded with the aim of overthrowing the July Monarchy. On 12 May 1839 the members of the Society tried to seize power in Paris by force, believing that a favourable situation existed for such action, since from 8 March 1839 France had been without a government following the resignation of a ministry headed by the Count Molé. The Hôtel de Ville was briefly occupied, a provisional government was proclaimed, and two days of street-fighting in the Saint-Denis and Saint Martin districts of Paris left over 100 people dead. However, the police and army remained loyal to the régime, the insurgents attracted little support, and moderate republicans immediately condemned the attempted *coup*. A court of the Chamber of Peers sentenced to death the leaders of the *coup*, Armand Barbès and Auguste Blanqui, but students and public figures such as Victor Hugo and Alphonse de Lamartine campaigned for clemency, and the sentences were commuted to life imprisonment.

The following year witnessed a second attempted *coup* by Louis Napoleon Bonaparte, who had left the United States for England. Undeterred by his failure at Strasbourg in 1836, and encouraged by the decision to rebury Napoleon's remains in Paris and by an outbreak of patriotic chauvinism over the possibility of French involvement in a conflict between Egypt and Turkey, Louis Napoleon Bonaparte and about fifty followers landed on the coast near Boulogne on 6 August 1840. The objectives were similar to those of 1836: the military garrisons of Boulogne and Lille were to be won over, the people were to be encouraged to rally to the Bonapartist cause, and after a triumphant march on Paris a Napoleonic régime was to be re-established. In fact the Boulogne garrison and National Guard, and even the local customs officers, resisted all seditious appeals; and the escapade rapidly ended in ignominious failure, with Louis Napoleon Bonaparte being rescued half-drowned from the sea. This time Louis Napoleon Bonaparte was tried by a court of the Chamber of Peers, like Barbès and Blanqui. He exploited the opportunity to present himself as representing the principle of popular sovereignty, the cause of the Empire, and the symbolic avenger of Waterloo, but this did not save him from a sentence of perpetual imprisonment.

Quite apart from Louis Napoleon Bonaparte's landing at Boulogne, 1840 seemed to be a year of crisis. A campaign for an extension of the parliamentary franchise, organized by the Paris moderate republican newspaper, *Le National*, and involving petitions and public banquets, helped to promote political discontent. The anniversary of the storming of the Bastille on 14 July became the focus of left-wing celebrations, some of which were officially banned. A commercial slump and high grain prices led to riots and strikes, including an incident in the provincial town of Foix in which thirteen demonstrators were killed. The government formed on 1 March 1840 and headed by Adolphe Thiers threatened to plunge France into war over a conflict in the Middle East and provoked a major parliamentary storm by a decision to construct a series of fortifications around Paris. There even occurred, on 15 October 1840, another attempt to assassinate Louis-Philippe. Meanwhile in September an Egyptian invasion of Lebanon and Syria, to which Thiers had given France's diplomatic support, had been checked at Beirut, partly through British intervention. With Britain, Austria and Russia prepared to give Turkey naval and military assistance, and with an explosion of chauvinism and francophobia in the German states, Thiers nevertheless stuck to his policy of backing Mehemet Ali, the ruler of Egypt. However Louis-Philippe, suspicious of Thiers and determined to avoid French involvement in an unnecessary war, rejected the draft submitted by Thiers for the Speech from the Throne at the opening of parliament, whereupon the Thiers government resigned (21 October). Eventually on 29 October Louis-Philippe appointed a new government nominally presided over by Marshal Soult, though in fact directed by the Minister of Foreign Affairs, François Guizot.

A Protestant intellectual from a comparatively modest provincial background, Guizot must often have seemed an unlikely custodian of the political fortunes of the July Monarchy. Yet for Louis-Philippe he had much to recommend him. Although he had served the Restoration Monarchy in various administrative posts and as a member of the Council of State, and had even attended Louis XVIII in exile during the Hundred Days, he had fallen victim to the right-wing reaction unleashed by the assassination of the Duke of Berry (13 February 1820). Deprived of his administrative post, of his membership of the Council of State, and even of his right to deliver university lectures, he had become a prominent figure in the liberal opposition; he had contributed articles to Le Globe, an important liberal newspaper; he had actively supported the liberal opposition political society, Aide-toi, le ciel t'aidera; and in January 1830 he had gained election to parliament as a liberal opposition deputy. During July and August 1830 he had emerged as one of the handful of politicians who successfully promoted the Orleanist solution to the constitutional crisis. Although his subsequent career had not been quite as prominent as might have been expected, he had headed the Ministry of the Interior during the potentially dangerous months following the July 1830 Revolution, he had introduced significant education reforms while Minister of Public Instruction (1832–7), and as ambassador in London (February–October 1840) he had demonstrated his commitment to peace and his ability to get on with the British at the time of the Mehemet Ali affair. Also, as a member of the Chamber of Deputies he had gained the reputation of being an effective debater and a skilful politician.

The formation of the Soult–Guizot government on 29 October 1840 marked a watershed in the history of the July Monarchy. In contrast to the previous decade, which had witnessed ministerial instability, a succession of crises and even the threat of war, there followed a period lasting at least until 1846 characterized by government stability, domestic calm and order, and peace for France abroad. Yet this period was to end with the dismissal of Guizot and with the overthrow of the Orleanist dynasty in the revolutionary upheaval of February 1848. Much of the responsibility for the initial apparent success and ultimate catastrophic failure of the Soult–Guizot government must rest with Guizot himself.   It has to be acknowledged that the task confronting Guizot was not easy, for his political position was weaker than it appeared to be. He did win the confidence and friendship of Louis-Philippe, but the monarch's increasing aversion to any significant reform and his contempt for any political opposition transformed their excellent personal relations into a liability as well as an asset. The recruitment of cabinet ministers who accepted his leadership, co-operated with government colleagues and were effective in office was always a problem for Guizot. The Chamber of Deputies, too, presented difficulties for him, since until the government successes in the general election of August 1846 he frequently could not be certain of a government majority. At the same time the years 1840 to 1846 witnessed a substantial increase in French industrial production, particularly in textiles and in metallurgical industries involved in the construction of new railway lines. This hitherto unprecedented industrial expansion helped to create severe social problems and to encourage a speculative boom, so that socially and economically France became very vulnerable to any economic recession. Guizot also suffered from a personal handicap in that parliament, the newspaper press and public opinion tended to be hostile to him, sometimes savagely so. His unpopularity doubtless had many causes. Physically unprepossessing, professorial in manner and apparently emotionally cold and rigorously intellectual, he lacked any personal warmth or charisma. For many Frenchmen his Protestantism and Geneva education, and his academic studies of English literature and of English history, were further counts against him. However, his unpopularity was above all a judgement on his policies as Minister of Foreign Affairs and as effective Prime Minister between October 1840 and February 1848.

As Minister of Foreign Affairs Guizot had to deal with the exceptionally sensitive issue of Anglo-French relations. Since 1815 politically conscious Frenchmen had tended to suffer from a sense of inferiority towards Britain and from a desire to reverse the verdict of Waterloo; and friction between France and Britain was likely to arise over a wide range of issues, including French expansion in Algeria and Morocco, conflicts of interest in Spain and Greece, the right of British warships to search French ships suspected of involvement in the slave trade, and colonial disputes arising from the proclamation of a French protectorate over the Pacific island of Tahiti. At first Guizot gave the impression of being subservient to Britain and of wanting peace at any price: he signed the Straits Convention of 13 July 1841 which settled the Mehemet Ali crisis; he conceded the 'right of search' to British warships in 1842; he agreed in September 1844 to pay an indemnity to George Pritchard, a British consul and Protestant missionary who had been expelled by the French from Tahiti; he accepted an Anglo-French treaty on the suppression of the slave trade (29 May 1845); and he helped to arrange three meetings between Louis-Philippe and Queen Victoria in 1843, 1844 and 1845. France needed to break out of the diplomatic isolation which had resulted from the reckless policies of Thiers, and a policy of Anglo-French co-operation was arguably eminently sensible and in the interests of both countries. However, such a policy was not popular in France. In particular, the decision to pay Pritchard an indemnity provoked stormy debates in parliament and for a time 'Pritchardiste' (or supporter of the indemnity) became the strongest abusive epithet in the French political vocabulary. Also the somewhat fragile *entente cordiale* formed between France and Britain by Guizot and Lord Aberdeen (British Foreign Secretary, 1841–6) did not survive the return of Lord Palmerston to the British Foreign Office in July 1846 or the arrangement the following month of a marriage between the heiress presumptive to the Spanish throne and the Duke of Montpensier, the youngest son of Louis-Philippe. Now Guizot stood accused of imperilling Anglo-French relations and French national interests for the sake of the dynastic ambitions of the House of Orleans; and the consequent rupture with Britain encouraged him to try to cultivate the northern Courts and to adopt more conservative foreign policies. Hence France did not protest vigorously when Austria in November 1846 annexed the Polish city of Cracow, in violation of the Treaties of 1815; and when in October 1847 a civil war broke out in Switzerland between a liberal majority in the Diet and a minority alliance of Catholic and conservative cantons known as the Sonderbund, Guizot supported the Sonderbund.

Guizot's domestic policies are usually labelled conservative, if not reactionary. In fact he was not incapable of introducing reforms. While Minister of Public Instruction he had been responsible for a law (28 June 1833) which had improved and extended primary education; and through his government's initiative parliament passed legislation regulating the use of child labour in factories (22 March 1841) and promoting the construction of railways (11 June 1842). However, essentially he believed in the maintenance of the *status quo*. As a Protestant bourgeois Guizot possessed no nostalgic sympathy for the Old Régime of pre-1789 France. Nevertheless, as someone whose father had been executed at the height of the Jacobin Terror in 1794 and who had succeeded through his own abilities and efforts, he had an exaggerated concern for order and stability and an exaggerated attachment to the virtues of property-ownership. Convinced that the July Monarchy, the Charter of 1830 and a parliament representing the property-owning classes were all indispensable for France, he showed little enthusiasm for any constitutional reform. Nor did he appreciate that France was experiencing profound social and economic changes which made his immobilism potentially dangerous. Ignoring the plight of those who lacked property and consequently the vote ('Get rich' being his unhelpful advice), he concentrated his political energies on maintaining the government's parliamentary majority and on winning parliamentary elections. Within this narrow sphere he achieved unprecedented success, particularly in securing a government majority of approximately 100 seats in the parliamentary general election of August 1846. Yet this triumph contributed to his political destruction. Guizot himself, who prior to August 1846 had avoided radical measures so as not to disturb his parliamentary majority, now believed that his large parliamentary majority made such measures unnecessary. At the same time his apparent permanence in political power encouraged some of his opponents to launch what became known as the reform banquet campaign.

Agitation to extend the parliamentary franchise, which restricted the vote to about 2.8 per cent of all adult male French citizens, had occurred throughout the reign of Louis-Philippe. Guizot's parliamentary successes, widely attributed to corruption, gave this agitation a new impetus. Between 1841 and 1847 eleven bills attempted to exclude government office-holders or 'fonctionnaires' from parliament; and in March 1847 even a moderate conservative deputy, Prosper Duvergier de Hauranne, introduced an electoral reform bill which would have halved the tax qualification for voters. The failure of all these measures encouraged a group of deputies, including Odilon Barrot and Duvergier de Hauranne, and a republican publisher, Charles Pagnerre, to launch an extra-parliamentary campaign, which, to avoid legal restrictions on public meetings, took the form of a series of political banquets. The first banquet, held in Paris on 9 July 1847, attracted some eighty deputies and over 1,000 other participants. Guizot's unpopularity, an economic recession following harvest failures in 1845 and 1846, the publication in 1847 of popular histories of the French Revolution favourable to republicanism by Louis Blanc, Jules Michelet and Lamartine, and a succession of scandals involving members of the Orleanist élite, all helped to create a climate favourable to the reform banquet campaign. Between August 1847 and February 1848 some sixty banquets were organized in provincial towns all over France; and Paris and

49

provincial newspapers fully reported the banquets and the accompanying speeches. At the same time the banquet campaign tended to become more radical. Toasts to the King were pointedly abandoned, while speakers demanded, not just parliamentary reform and an extension of the franchise, but the introduction of manhood suffrage and socialist policies.

During the summer and autumn of 1847 the Guizot government did not respond in any significant way to the reform banquet campaign, though local officials sometimes obstructed the holding of banquets. However, when parliament reassembled for the new session on 28 December 1847 Louis-Philippe in his Speech from the Throne branded the reform banquet campaign as an 'agitation fomenting blind and hostile passions'. This description of a peaceful protest in pursuit of constitutional reform was imprudently provocative, particularly since petitions, votes in the general councils of fifteen departments, by-election results and the attitude of numerous newspapers all indicated the widespread support for the campaign and the extent of the government's unpopularity, even among the propertied classes.

The official banquet campaign petered out with the new parliamentary session, but a group of officers of the National Guard legion for the twelfth *arrondissement* of Paris formed a committee to organize a reform banquet. Alarmed by the prospect of political violence in one of the poorest and most radical districts of the capital, on 14 January 1848 the government prohibited the proposed banquet. However, the committee remained resolutely determined to challenge this ban and to assert the right of assembly. A large number of opposition deputies, who supported this attitude but who wanted a less radical banquet, helped to form a new committee which planned to hold a banquet in Paris on 22 February. On the morning of 21 February Paris opposition newspapers published details of the demonstration which was to accompany this banquet the following day, including an invitation to National Guardsmen to participate in uniform. Regarding this as an unacceptable provocation, the government immediately banned the banquet and the demonstration. Hastily summoned meetings of opposition deputies and of the banquet committee agreed to accept this ban.

Undeterred by the capitulation of opposition deputies and by the cancellation of the twelfth *arrondissement* banquet, large numbers of Paris National Guardsmen, students and workers joined street demonstrations in central Paris during 22 February. When soldiers and police attempted to clear the streets, the demonstrators reacted violently by ransacking gunsmiths' shops and by constructing street barricades. Early in the morning of 23 February a mobilization of the National Guard was ordered, but most Guardsmen supported the reform movement and were not prepared to risk their lives for the Guizot government. Consequently the army and the police again had to face violent demonstrators, who attacked police stations and erected street barricades. At last alarmed by the situation, Louis-Philippe dismissed Guizot during the afternoon of 23 February. The dismissal of Guizot, and the failure to form a new ministry under Molé, Thiers or Odilon Barrot, left the King without a government at a time when violent incidents were occurring in many parts of Paris. In the most serious of those incidents, between eight and nine in the evening of 23 February soldiers guarding the Ministry of Foreign Affsairs in the Boulevard des Capucines panicked and fired into a crowd of demonstrators, killing fifty-two and wounding many more. Some of the dead were piled onto a cart which was dragged through popular districts of Paris. This macabre funeral cortège, illuminated by torches, together with rumours that the government had ordered a general massacre of the people, spontaneously provoked a massive popular uprising. During the night of 23–4 February the construction of innumerable barricades transformed the popular districts of Paris into a series of fortresses and cut off isolated police and army units. As dawn broke on 24 February violence erupted on an even greater scale: police stations and army barracks were besieged and their occupants disarmed; prisons were broken into and prisoners liberated; and vigorous resistance frustrated an offensive operation ordered by the new army commander, Marshal Bugeaud, to remove some of the barricades. Emboldened by their successes, crowds of demonstrators overran the Hôtel de Ville and the Palais Royal and began to surround the Tuilieries. Uncertain of the loyalty of the solders and National Guardsmen defending the palace, and frightened of the consequences of a protracted struggle, at about noon on 24 February 1848 Louis-Philippe wrote out his abdication.

4 The June Days

An analysis of the February Days, during which Louis-Philippe was overthrown and the Second Republic proclaimed, is essential for an understanding of the development of the 1848 Revolution in France and for the outbreak of the Parisian insurrection known as the June Days. The February Days came as the unexpected climax to the long-drawn-out reform banquet campaign (July 1847–February 1848). The original organizers of this campaign had wanted reform, not revolution: the elimination of '*fonctionnaires*' from the Chamber of Deputies and an extension of the parliamentary franchise so as to create a constitutional system which would be less susceptible to government corruption and more representative of public opinion, a constitutional system, it was believed, that would not produce a Guizot ministry. Subscription costs and practical factors restricted the number and social composition of those who actually dined at these reform banquets. However, particularly since the banquets were often held on Sundays, workers could participate as spectators; and newspapers extensively reported the proceedings of the sixty-odd banquets, which were held all over France. Moreover, the reluctance of some of Guizot's parliamentary opponents to join the campaign, on the grounds of its dubious legal and political character, meant that more radical figures, either local or national, took over a number of banquets and gained a platform for their views.[7] A group of National Guard officers originally planned the twelfth *arrondissement* banquet as a radical banquet, but, following the first ban on the banquet imposed by the Prefect of Police (14 January 1848), a new organizing committee took over. This committee, dominated by opposition deputies, wanted an orderly and peaceful protest and to that end prepared detailed instructions for the parade that was to precede the banquet on 22 February. When the Prefect of Police banned the banquet and the accompanying demonstration for the second time, because the parade instructions published in four opposition newspapers on 21 February had included an invitation to National Guardsmen to participate in uniform, a meeting of opposition deputies voted not to attend the banquet or the parade. This led the organizing committee to cancel the twelfth *arrondissement* banquet.

The reform banquet campaign produced the political crisis which provoked the 1848 Revolution in France, but only because three days of street-fighting in Paris followed the cancellation of the twelfth *arrondissement* banquet. On 22 February, unlike the bourgeois opposition leaders, large numbers of Paris workers were not prepared to submit to the Guizot government, and took to the streets in violent protest. By the beginning of 1848 Paris and its suburbs had a population of approximately one and a quarter million. The bulk of this population was, by contemporary definitions, poor: in 1846 72 per cent of all Parisian tenants were exempted from payment of the minimum rent tax, because their rents were so low; and during the ten years prior to 1848 nearly 80 per cent of Parisian dead were buried in paupers' graves. The Parisian poor tended to live in over-crowded housing in the eastern half of the capital, and were mainly building workers, domestic servants and skilled artisans producing in small craft workshops a wide variety of textiles, clothes, shoes, furniture, luxury goods and metalwork. Although Paris wage rates exceeded those in the provinces, the cost of living was also higher and few Paris workers could afford to save or to insure themselves. Inadequate cereal harvests in 1845 and 1846, and the failure of the potato crop in 1846, resulted in a long period of high prices for the staple food items of the urban poor. Also, two consecutive years of bad harvests sharply reduced the demand for consumer goods, causing a severe business slump, which for the urban poor meant an enormous increase in unemployment. By the beginning of 1848 at least half the working-class population of Paris lacked employment and many of the remainder had to work part-time. It is difficult to be precise about the political consciousness of Paris workers before the February Days. They were denied any active political role; working-class political clubs and societies had been virtually suppressed; and the three newspapers which specifically catered for the Paris working class had circulations of 1,000 or less. Nevertheless, it is probably safe to assume that for many Paris workers Louis-Philippe and Guizot represented oppressive class rule, a callous indifference to the sufferings of the poor, and the betrayal of France's republican and revolutionary traditions. Although not politically organized, or even widely politically conscious, before the February Days, Paris workers had the potential to play an important political role. Migration patterns and life expectancy rates meant that a large proportion of the Parisian working class was aged between twenty and forty. Unlike their provincial counterparts, the vast majority of these workers, both men and women, could read and write. Concentrated in enormous numbers in the nation's capital, and struggling for survival in very difficult circumstances, the workers of Paris not surprisingly took to the streets in their tens of thousands when a political crisis coincided with an economic recession of exceptional severity.

The success of the revolutionary movement during the February

Days can be attributed, not just to the massive contribution of Paris workers, but also to the intervention of students, to the behaviour of the Paris National Guard, and to the response of the Orleanist régime. The University of Paris and the Grandes Ecoles, or élite professional training institutions, attracted large numbers of students to the capital. Although they mostly came from bourgeois backgrounds, many students opposed Guizot, particularly his foreign policies, and supported the reform banquet campaign. A group of Paris students even planned to hold their own reform banquet in January or February 1848. At the beginning of January 1848 the government suspended Michelet, a popular professor at the Collège de France. His dismissal for political reasons, following the similar dismissals of Mickiewicz and Quinet, led to anti-government demonstrations and protests, which were organized by two student newspapers, *La Lanterne du Quartier latin* and *L'Avant-Garde*. These newspapers also encouraged and directed student participation in the February Days.

In Paris the defence of the régime and the maintenance of law and order were partly the responsibility of the National Guard, which the July Monarchy had re-established along remarkably democratic lines. A law of 22 March 1831 removed all property qualifications for entry into the Guard and established promotion by election. In the various Paris disturbances of the 1831 to 1835 period the National Guard performed reasonably well. However, after 1835 morale declined as the institution became a popular target for ridicule and fears of an attempt to assassinate Louis-Philippe ended all royal reviews. Many members of the Paris National Guard must have shared the widespread detestation of Guizot and must have suffered from the economic recession which began in 1845. Since most of them could not vote in parliamentary elections they generally supported the reform banquet campaign, and National Guard officers initiated the twelfth *arrondissement* banquet. Consequently, during the February Days few Guardsmen were prepared to fight effectively to defend Guizot or even Louis-Philippe, while many actually joined the insurgents.

The response of the Orleanist régime can be faulted throughout the crisis. The comparatively good harvests of 1847 and consequent fall in food prices encouraged a belief that the worst of the economic recession was over, whereas in fact the urban poor faced a deteriorating employment situation. A similar official complacency prevailed regarding the reform banquet campaign, since an earlier campaign had failed in 1840 and Louis-Philippe felt secure with the Guizot government and its parliamentary majority. The submission of the Algerian leader Abd-el-Kader at the end of December 1847 was expected to improve the régime's prestige and popularity. In fact this success had little domestic impact in France, unlike the provocative language of the Speech from the Throne and the attacks directed against the government in the subsequent parliamentary debates. The last-minute cancellation of the twelfth *arrondissement* banquet virtually guaranteed disturbances, for which no adequate military preparations had been made. As the Parisian insurrection developed Guizot's dismissal on 23 February effectively deprived Louis-Philippe of a government, while the appointment of Marshal Bugeaud as commander-in-chief of all forces in Paris early in the morning of 24 February was unwise in view of Bugeaud's unpopularity (he had been the jailer of the Duchess of Berry and was held responsible for the Rue Transnonain massacre of April 1834). In any case, by the morning of 24 February a desperate military situation confronted the Orleanist régime: the police had virtually been eliminated; the National Guard were either unreliable or disloyal; and much of the army garrison, cut off by street barricades from orders, ammunition, food and shelter from the rain, had become demoralized and ineffective. Finally, Louis-Philippe's abdication around noon on 24 February amounted to the resignation of the régime. From some provincial base he could have attempted to rally support, but he was too old and dispirited for such an enterprise, nor did he want to start a civil war. He therefore fled from the Tuileries with his family and escaped to England in disguise.

Louis-Philippe's abdication created a power vacuum. His eldest son had died accidentally in July 1842, so he abdicated in favour of his nine-year-old grandson, the Count of Paris. To assert the claims of her son, the Duchess of Orleans left the Tuileries for the Chamber of Deputies, where Dupin and Odilon Barrot proposed that the Count of Paris should be recognized as King with the Duchess of Orleans as Regent. This proposal encountered vigorous opposition from both Legitimists (Genoude, La Rochejaquelein and Berryer), who wanted a national referendum, and from other opposition deputies (Marie, Crémieux, Ledru-Rollin and Lamartine), who demanded a provisional government. During the debate crowds of demonstrators, many of them armed and in a triumphant and revolutionary spirit after the capture of the Tuileries, invaded the Chamber of Deputies, where their presence virtually guaranteed the rejection of the regency, the flight of the Duchess of Orleans, and the proclamation of a provisional government. At a series of meetings at the editorial office of the main moderate republican newspaper of Paris, *Le National*, an agreed list of members for the provisional government had been drawn up. Lamartine, Dupont de l'Eure and Ledru-Rollin announced the names on this list in the Chamber to popular acclamation, and then proceeded to the Hôtel de Ville to establish this new government for France.

The Provisional Government proclaimed in the Chamber of Deputies during the afternoon of 24 February consisted of Dupont de l'Eure, Garnier-Pagès and Marie (all moderate republicans), François Arago (a left-wing scientist who had accepted the constitutional monarchy), Crémieux (a liberal monarchist), Lamartine (a major literary and political figure who had joined the opposition in 1843) and Ledru-Rollin (a left-wing republican and co-founder of *La Réforme*). As deputies they had all been prominent opponents of Guizot: Crémieux, Dupont de l'Eure, Garnier-Pagès and Ledru-Rollin had delivered important speeches at reform banquets; the most resolute supporters of the twelfth *arrondissement* banquet had included Crémieux, Dupont de l'Eure, Lamartine, Ledru-Rollin and Marie; and Crémieux, Lamartine, Ledru-Rollin and Marie had insisted on a provisional government in the parliamentary debate of 24 February. After they had all assembled at the Hôtel de Ville they formed a government with François Arago as Minister of the Navy, Crémieux as Minister of Justice, Dupont de l'Eure as President, Garnier-Pagès as, successively, Mayor of Paris and Minister of Finance, Lamartine as Minister of Foreign Affairs, Ledru-Rollin as Minister of the Interior, and Marie as Minister of Public Works. After these ministerial posts had been allocated a delegation from the left-wing republican newspaper, *La Réforme*, confronted the Provisional Government and insisted on the inclusion in the government of two prominent left-wing figures, Louis Blanc and Flocon, together with a worker known as Albert, and Marrast, editor of *Le National*. Anxious to avoid antagonizing the radicals, particularly as the Hôtel de Ville had been invaded by demonstrators, the Provisional Government admitted them, though they were at first officially designated as secretaries.

The Provisional Government constituted essentially a coalition of moderate republicans and left-wing republicans, with the moderate republicans in a strong majority. As François Arago, Crémieux and Lamartine usually sided with the moderate republicans, the only left-wing republicans in the government were Albert, Louis Blanc, Flocon and Ledru-Rollin; and of these, only Ledru-Rollin gained a ministerial post, though admittedly this was the crucially important Ministry of the Interior. Similarly, moderate republicans dominated the posts held by those outside the Provisional Government, with the exception of the Post Office and the Prefecture of Police, where radicals had occupied the buildings and installed Etienne Arago and Caussidière respectively. Moderate republicans believed in manhood suffrage, equality before the law, freedom of expression and association, and in a republican constitution. Opposed to political violence, they considered that manhood suffrage would provide the key to unlocking peaceful political change. Left-wing republicans maintained that social and economic reforms should precede or accompany political reforms, and some left-wing republicans were prepared on occasion to accept or condone political violence. Moderate republicans and left-wing republicans had disagreed publicly and frequently before 1848, but the reform banquet campaign, the political eclipse of figures such as Odilon Barrot and Adolphe Thiers, and the revolutionary upheaval of the February Days, had swept both moderate republicans and left-wing republicans to power. However, the strong majority position of the moderate republicans meant that government policies were unlikely to have a radical character, which helps to explain the popular frustration in Paris that eventually exploded in the June insurrection.

The Provisional Government at once had to decide whether or not to proclaim a republic. Louis Blanc, Flocon and Ledru-Rollin argued forcibly that a republic should be proclaimed at once without any reservations, as the demonstrators surrounding and invading the Hôtel de Ville repeatedly insisted. However, the Provisional Government lacked any constitutional mandate for such a decision, which threatened provincial opposition and foreign hostility. After heated discussion the Provisional Government agreed to declare in its first official proclamation that it wanted the republic, provided this were accepted by the people, who would be immediately consulted. There followed government decrees dissolving the Chamber of Peers and the Chamber of Deputies, and setting free all political prisoners. The decree dissolving the Chamber of Deputies declared that a National Assembly would be summoned as soon as the Provisional Government could guarantee the public order essential to an election.

The change of régime encountered no significant public opposition in France and the transfer of power was accomplished remarkably smoothly. In contrast to the aftermath of the Revolution of 1830, few officials or office-holders resigned their posts, while many offered to serve the Provisional Government. This reflected an absence of personal loyalty to Louis-Philippe and conservative fears that any opposition might undermine government authority and encourage revolutionary violence. The sudden, unexpected and complete collapse of the July Monarchy, which had ruled France for over seventeen years, the triumph of popular violence and of a revolutionary movement in Paris, and further violence such as the destruction of the royal château at Neuilly, the burning of the Rothschild mansion at Suresnes, and the sabotage of railway lines around Paris, all tended to panic the wealthier classes. However, a fear of a repetition of the Jacobin dictatorship and terror of 1793 manifested itself, not in resistance, but in apparent support for the revolution: the wealthier classes contributed with uncharacteristic generosity to public subscriptions for the victims of the February Days and volunteered in large numbers to enrol in the National Guard. Administrative authority in the provinces was peacefully surrendered by prefects and sub-prefects to self-appointed committees, composed of local opponents of Guizot and, to a lesser extent, of republicans. Provincial outbreaks of violence occurred only in a few urban centres, such as Lyons, Lille and Rouen, where the causes seem to have been as much economic and social as political.

Nevertheless, from the outset the Provisional Government faced an extremely difficult task. The Second Republic had been proclaimed, but its character had yet to be determined, in very unfavourable circumstances. Orleanist officials and office-holders clearly lacked any genuine commitment to republicanism, so they fell victim to wholesale dismissals, which inevitably caused much resentment and could result in the appointment and promotion of the unknown, inexperienced and incompetent. The absence of much popular violence after the February Days, the prominent position of Lamartine, an aristocratic land-owner, in the Provisional Government, and the relative moderation of government policies, helped to reassure the wealthier classes but did not prevent a run on the banks, numerous bankruptcies and a general collapse of financial confidence. Relative over-population, the loss of communal rights, chronic peasant indebtedness, low prices for agricultural products, and the general economic recession affecting most cottage industries, promoted discontent in many rural areas, the control of which led to the deployment of 48,000 troops between February and June 1848. In the towns unemployment, aggravated by the financial crisis and the disruption of foreign trade, remained the overriding problem and constituted an impetus to popular violence, at first usually directed against machines and foreign workers. Especially critical, for the Provisional Government, was the situation in Paris. The government lacked any effective military force, with the demoralization and disorganization of the National Guard, and of the regular troops in the Paris area, and with the withdrawal of most regular army units from central Paris immediately after 24 February. At the same time a triumphant and revolutionary crowd besieged the Hôtel de Ville, insisting on a radical and socialist republic. In particular the crowd demanded that the Provisional Government should provide employment, guarantee the right to work and adopt the red flag as France's national flag.

Within the Provisional Government several members, notably Louis Blanc, wanted to introduce a socialist programme, and the Provisional Government remained defenceless against the revolutionary crowd. The Provisional Government therefore decreed on 25 February that it promised a living wage to every worker and employment to all male citizens, and that it recognized that workers should form associations amongst themselves to secure the legitimate reward of their labour. Also, workers were allocated the former royal civil list. The following day the immediate establishment of National Workshops was decreed, to provide government-financed work for the unemployed. These measures did not satisfy many Paris workers, who wanted a government minstry which would intervene in the economy and government direction of the labour force; and on 28 February several thousand Paris workers demonstrated for a 'Ministry of Progress' and for the 'Organization of Labour'. In response the Provisional Government decided that a commission of workers' representatives should meet under the chairmanship of Louis Blanc in the Luxembourg Palace (the former Chamber of Peers), to discuss workers' grievances and how to remedy them. Meanwhile on 25 and 26 February demonstrators at the Hôtel de Ville had demanded that the government should adopt the red flag. The principle of changing the national flag when the régime changed had been followed in 1789, 1814, 1815 and 1830. However the adoption of the red flag, a symbol of radicalism, would have been regarded as a capitulation to popular militancy and as the precursor of extreme left-wing government policies. Consequently, the government's refusal to adopt the red flag was of considerable symbolic significance.

Having survived its first days in power the Provisional Government proceeded to implement the programme of moderate republicanism. Two very important humanitarian measures were introduced, the abolition of the death penalty for political offences (26 February) and the abolition of slavery in all of France's colonies and overseas possessions (4 March and 27 April). The proclamation of the principle of parliamentary elections on the basis of direct manhood suffrage (2 March) and the annulment of the September 1835 press laws (6 March) comprised the chief political reforms. Social and economic reforms were less dramatic and at least partly a response to pressure from Paris radicals and workers. Following representations from Louis Blanc and the Luxembourg Commission, the exploitation of sweated labour by sub-contractors was prohibited and the maximum working day limited to ten hours in Paris and eleven hours in the provinces (2 March). Other measures included the establishment of discount banks, the ending of imprisonment for debt, and the funding of public expenditure on railways, public buildings and street improvements. Confronted by a difficult financial situation, the Provisional Government pursued orthodox fiscal policies. Anxious to restore confidence, the government wanted to balance income and expenditure. The government could not borrow significant sums because of the general economic crisis and the political uncertainties, and it decided not to sell off major state assets such as forests. Consequently, taxation had to be increased. For social and political reasons a redistribution of the tax burden was attempted, with the removal of taxes on alcoholic drinks, the promise to suppress the salt tax, and the imposition of new taxes on expensive rented property, luxury carriages and male domestic servants. However, the principal fiscal measure was the decision taken on 16 March to increase the main tax on property by a massive 45 per cent, thereby creating what became known as the 45 centimes tax.

The ending of all restrictions on public meetings and demonstrations, and the freeing of the newspaper press from censorship, restrictive laws and the stamp tax, encouraged the emergence of numerous newspapers and political clubs, particularly in Paris. Many of these newspapers and clubs demanded the adoption of more radical government policies, such as the improvement of educational opportunities for the poor, the dissolution of capitalist monopolies, the promotion of co-operative workshops, the nationalization of mines, railways, banks and insurance companies, and the discouragement of profiteering by speculators and middlemen through the introduction of schemes whereby goods could be bartered directly by producers and consumers. Many Parisian radicals and workers believed that such reforms should be introduced before the holding of a general election for a new national parliament. However on 5 March the Provisional Government announced that elections for a National Assembly would be held on 9 April, while elections to fill the officer ranks of the rapidly expanding Paris National Guard were scheduled for 18 March. As early as 4 March Auguste Blanqui's Central Republican Society (the first and initially the most prestigious of the Paris revolutionary clubs of 1848) voted to demand that the Provisional Government should postpone the National Assembly elections. Blanqui wanted a three-month postponement on the grounds that the country was not ready for elections since for the previous fifty years only the Counter-Revolution had had an effective voice in France. Following the rejection of Blanqui's petition by the Provisional Government on 7 March the protest movement broadened; and by 16 March a number of Paris clubs had agreed to organize a mass demonstration to press for the postponement of the National Guard and National Assembly elections, and, in addition, the exclusion of all regular soldiers from central Paris. Simultaneously the Provisional Government, and particularly Ledru-Rollin, antagonized the more conservative elements in Paris: Ledru-Rollin as Minister of the Interior issued a circular, published on 12 March, informing *commissaires* sent to administer the departments in the place of prefects that their powers were unlimited, and should be used to secure the election of good republicans to the National Assembly; the publication began on 13 March of a series of official *Bulletins of the Republic*, which were designed to win support for left-wing republicanism in the forthcoming elections; and on 14 March the government ordered the dissolution of the élite companies of the Paris National Guard. All this provoked what has been described as 'the first feeble attempt at counter-revolution since February'[8] – a protest demonstration outside the Hôtel de Ville by several thousand National Guardsmen on 16 March. The following day Paris radicals organized a massive counter-demonstration.

After the February Days all regular army units had been withdrawn from central Paris, apart from two cavalry regiments and several artillery batteries, which remained at the Ecole Militaire, the largest barracks in Paris. The task of policing Paris fell mainly on the National Guard, the paper strength of which increased from about 57,000 in February to approximately 190,000 by mid-March. In addition to the National Guard, a part-time volunteer militia, the Provisional Government formed various paramilitary units, the members of which were paid and full-time: the Republican Guard, a small force recruited from those who had captured the Hôtel de Ville on 24 February; the Popular Guard of Montagnards, a force of some 500 to 600 men organized by Caussidière, the Prefect of Police; and the Mobile National Guard, which by mid-May comprised over 16,000 men, mostly unemployed Parisians aged between sixteen and thirty, many of whom had fought on the barricades in February. Uncertain of the political loyalties of these newly formed and expanded paramilitary units, the Provisional Government wanted to re-establish the regular army garrison of Paris and announced modest plans for doing so on 14 March. Those plans were overtaken by the events of 16 and 17 March. The National Guard demonstration of 16 March almost amounted to a mutiny while the popular demonstration of 17 March threatened the very survival of the Provisional Government. The demonstration's enormous size (possibly over 100,000 participated) caught the government unprepared and unprotected, so that it had to meet in the Hôtel de Ville about forty delegates representing the various clubs and organizations taking part in the demonstration. A petition was read out demanding the withdrawal of regular troops from Paris, and the postponement of elections to 5 April for the National Guard and to 31 May for the National Assembly. While stressing its need for independence, the Provisional Government had to concede the withdrawal of the residue of the regular army garrison from central Paris and the postponement of the elections, from 18 March to 5 April for the National Guard and from 9 to 23 April for the National Assembly.

In the elections to fill the officer ranks of the Paris National Guard held between 5 and 10 April radical and left-wing candidates tended to fare badly. Partly to compensate for this it was agreed that workers belonging to the organized trades represented in the Luxembourg Commission would elect fourteen candidates to serve as staff officers in the Paris National Guard. Workers voted in person at the Champs de Mars (roughly where the Eiffel Tower now stands) on Sunday 16 April. After the vote a large number of workers decided to march on the Hôtel de Ville to impose a more radical programme on the Provisional Government. There seem to have been specific demands for a purge of moderates from the government and for a Ministry of Progress headed by Louis Blanc. Warned in advance, the Provisional Government was relatively well prepared for the demonstration, and a mobilization of the National Guard elicited a good response, so that when the demonstrators arrived at the Hôtel de Ville they found it surrounded by Guardsmen. This constituted a major set-back for the Paris revolutionary movement. A previously planned military parade in Paris on 20 April became almost a celebration of the government and of its confidence in the National Guard; and the prestige of the moderate republicans in the Provisional Government was enhanced just before the National Assembly elections of 23 April.

The National Assembly elections of 23 April 1848 were the first parliamentary elections ever held in any major state by direct manhood suffrage. Each department was a single constituency, with the 900 seats in the Assembly being distributed on the basis of one representative for every 40,000 inhabitants. Every male French citizen aged twenty-one or over could vote for the total number of representatives for his department. Any male French citizen aged twenty-five or over was eligible for election, and each elected representative qualified for a payment of twenty-five francs per day during the parliamentary session. Electoral corruption had been one of the principal charges levelled against Guizot, so it is perhaps not surprising that the Provisional Government decided not to give its official endorsement to any candidate, though government members, as citizens, could make individual recommendations. However, Ledru-Rollin, the Minister of the Interior, did try to promote the election of republican candidates and the dissemination of republican propaganda through the electoral influence of his *commissaires* and through the distribution of official bulletins. Similarly, Carnot, the Minister of Public Instruction, circulated republican literature to primary school teachers. While a significant number of *commissaires* stood successfully as candidates, attempts to spread republican propaganda and to mobilize primary school teachers seem to have had little influence or even to have been counter-productive.

In the absence of any clear or effective direction from the Provisional Government a rather confused electoral campaign developed, with much apparent overlap of electoral support and political ideology. Independently from the Provisional Government a group of moderate republicans formed at the beginning of March a central committee, which chose a list of thirty-four candidates to represent the department of the Seine and which approved lists of recommended candidates for nearly all the provincial departments, lists which *Le National* and several provincial newspapers printed. The list for the Seine included all members of the Provisional Government, though on 23 April *Le National* suggested alternatives for Albert, Louis Blanc, Flocon and Ledru-Rollin. Moderate republican newspapers tended to urge the electorate to support republicanism, the record of the Provisional Government and the rights of workers and peasants, but also the maintenance of law and order and the protection of the institutions of the family and private property.

The electoral campaigning of the radicals concentrated on Paris, though left-wing Paris clubs did dispatch emissaries into the provinces (apparently to little effect), while the left-wing newspaper, *La Commune de Paris*, and the relatively small number of provincial left-wing newspapers, did recommend some candidates in the provinces. In Paris the Luxembourg Commission and the main left-wing newspapers backed the candidatures of Albert, Louis Blanc, Flocon and Ledru-Rollin, and of various radicals. However, no agreed list of left-wing candidates for the department of the Seine emerged, and in the provinces some candidates who were clearly not left-wing nevertheless received left-wing endorsement. Left-wing newspapers declared they wanted the election of 'genuine' republicans and, invoking the memory of 1793, argued for economic, social and educational reforms. Altogether the electoral campaign indicated the disunity of the Left and its limited influence, even in Paris.

Conservatives, having recovered from the shock of the February Days, were able to exploit the advantages which their wealth, social status and political experience gave them. They, too, formed electoral committees, and many conservative newspapers printed lists of recommended candidates. The moderate republican members of the Provisional Government headed the lists of candidates backed by conservative newspapers in the department of the Seine; and, with no bar on multiple candidatures, conservatives supported prominent moderate republicans, particularly Lamartine, in several provincial departments. This reflected, not so much a conservative conversion to moderate republicanism, as a conservative belief that support for the moderate republicans would keep the Left at bay and that Lamartine constituted Ledru-Rollin's main opponent within the Provisional Government. Similarly, few conservative candidates publicly opposed republicanism, presenting themselves instead as defenders of order, property, family, religion, and of the national interests of France.

In the parliamentary general election of 23 April conservative candidates were stunningly successful. The elected representatives included some 439 who can be classified as conservatives as against 230 moderate republicans and fifty-five radicals and socialists. While only nineteen former parliamentary supporters of Guizot were elected in April, conservatives who had previously accepted the July Monarchy and never associated themselves with republicanism gained a clear majority. In social terms, agricultural land-owners and professional men, particularly lawyers, dominated the National Assembly, in which seventy-five ex-peers or nobles sat, but only seven foremen, seventeen workers and no peasants. Thus the impact of the February Revolution and the introduction of manhood suffrage had surprisingly little influence on the results of the elections. The elections themselves took place in a calm and orderly manner almost everywhere in France, with an apparent minimum of corruption and with a very high turn-out of over 80 per cent of the electorate. Local notables, who had monopolized parliamentary politics under the July Monarchy, seem to have effectively reasserted their political power and influence which the February Days had temporarily effaced. The Roman Catholic Church, which had at first almost welcomed the Revolution, with bishops ordering masses to be celebrated in memory of the victims of the February Days and with priests blessing newly planted trees of liberty, had rapidly rediscovered its traditional fears of republicanism thanks to Ledru-Rollin, Carnot and the radical Left. Consequently, the Catholic bishops and clergy tended to urge the faithful to vote for conservative candidates in the April elections. The elections happened to coincide with Easter Sunday, and contemporaries reported that parish priests led voters from the church to the polling booth. Altogether the conservative influence of the Catholic Church seems to have been significant in several departments, notably in Brittany. Peasants, who comprised the vast majority of the electorate, apparently reacted against the popular violence, increased taxation and interference from Paris with which they had come to associate republicanism and the radical Left. Also, conservatives could generally field better-known candidates, tended to subscribe to a vote-catching programme and in many departments formed a sensible tactical alliance with moderate republicans, while republicans, especially left-wing republicans, suffered from bad organization, even in Paris, and gave the impression of being indifferent towards peasant grievances.

The National Assembly first met in Paris on 4 May in a hastily constructed chamber in the courtyard of the old parliament building. After a ceremonial opening, the Assembly confirmed the proclamation of the Republic and then heard reports from Lamartine and other members of the Provisional Government justifying their tenure of office, reports which won a congratulatory vote from the Assembly. The principal legislative task facing the Assembly was the drawing up of a new constitution for France, but in the meantime it had to approve another interim government. In the course of discussions two main proposals emerged: the direct election by the Assembly either of all members of the government or of just an executive commission, which would in turn appoint government ministers. The moderate republicans, who had predominated in the Provisional Government, wanted to remain in power, and thus favoured an executive commission which they would monopolize and which would enable them to fill most of the ministerial posts. Conservatives tended to prefer a government directly elected by the Assembly and to demand the exclusion of all radicals and socialists from office. However, conservatives were not yet ready to exploit their majority position in the Assembly; and they had to take account of Lamartine, who had come first in the Seine elections and who had polled some 1,283,500 votes in ten departments. Like the moderate republicans, Lamartine wanted an executive commission, but unlike most of them he insisted that the executive commission should include Ledru-Rollin, the most prominent left-wing republican. Lamartine had disagreed publicly with Ledru-Rollin over the powers of *commissaires* and the use of official bulletins for electoral purposes, but he seems to have enjoyed quite good personal relations with Ledru-Rollin at this time and to have believed that the radical Left should be represented in the government, if only to defuse potential left-wing violence. The Assembly grudgingly accepted Lamartine's demands. A vote of 411 to 385 rejected the proposal for a government directly elected by the Assembly; and the Assembly voted for a five-member executive commission, though Lamartine received fewer votes than his colleagues François Arago, Garnier-Pagès and Marie, with Ledru-Rollin trailing a long way behind.

The Executive Commission suffered from severe handicaps from the day of its formation on 10 May. The conservative majority in the National Assembly had little reason to support a government in which conservatives remained totally unrepresented. Moreover, many conservatives had voted for Lamartine in April so as to vote against the Left, only to witness Lamartine using his popular mandate to force the Assembly to accept Ledru-Rollin's inclusion in the Executive Commission. Also, the Executive Commission appointed Flocon, a left-wing republican, to be Minister of Agriculture and Commerce, and allowed the radical Caussidière to retain the Prefecture of Police. At the same time the radical Left felt betrayed and frustrated: the hopes aroused by the February Revolution had been dashed with the intensification of urban unemployment, the cautious moderation of government policies and the conservative successes in the April elections. Radical anger at the election results exploded into popular violence in Limoges and Rouen at the end of April, while in Paris a major confrontation became virtually inevitable.

Exaggerated reports of 'the massacre of Rouen' intensified the widespread sense of grievance and frustration among Paris radicals and workers, as did the exclusion of Albert and Louis Blanc from the new administration and the Assembly's rejection on 10 May of Louis Blanc's proposals for a Ministry of Progress and of Wolowski's pleas for help for the beleaguered Poles. The cause of Polish independence, popular in France since 1815, had after February 1848 been enthusiastically embraced by the radical Parisian Left. News of Prussian repression in Posen and of an Austrian bombardment of Cracow prompted the Committee of Polish Emigration in Paris to appeal to the Paris clubs at the beginning of May to support a mass lobbying of the National Assembly for French arms and assistance for the Poles. The left-wing Paris clubs responded favourably, since not only was Poland a popular cause, but also a pro-Polish demonstration could serve as a means of reviving their flagging political influence and of challenging the government and the Assembly. After the Assembly had rejected the motions of Louis Blanc and Wolowski a group of radicals around the club leader Sobrier seems to have plotted a *coup d'état* to coincide with the Polish demonstration. However, the large crowd of demonstrators which marched from the Place de la Bastille to the Assembly on 15 May was largely unarmed. Owing to a series of miscalculations and misunderstandings, the National Guard failed to prevent the demonstrators from invading the Assembly. For three traumatic hours, graphically described in de Tocqueville's memoirs, hordes of demonstrators paralysed the Assembly and intimidated the representatives. The sound of drums being beaten to mobilize the National Guard apparently encouraged one leading demonstrator. Huber, to declare the dissolution of the Assembly, after which Albert and Barbès led a mass of demonstrators to the Hôtel de Ville to establish a self-proclaimed provisional government, while other radicals tried to occupy various government buildings. This attempt to repeat the events of 24 February rapidly ended in failure as the National Guard, after its belated mobilization, cleared the Assembly and the Hôtel de Ville and generally restored order.

While virtually no loss of life occurred in Paris on 15 May, the events of that day had a profound political impact. The government, shaken by what had happened and desperately concerned to restore its authority and credibility, for the first time since 24 February openly resorted to repression in Paris: the left-wing Paris clubs suffered various forms of official harassment and radical leaders, such as Albert, Barbès, Blanqui, Raspail and Sobrier, were arrested and imprisoned. To strengthen its military capabilities, the government reorganized the command structure of the National Guard and reintroduced a large regular army garrison into central Paris. The conservative majority in the National Assembly, furious at the attack on their dignity and sovereignty, blamed the Assembly's invasion on the incompetence of the Executive Commission and on the treasonable behaviour of various left-wing figures: they forced Caussidière to resign from the Prefecture of Police; they in effect put Louis Blanc on trial; and they ceased to treat the members of the Executive Commission with respect. For the Paris popular movement, 15 May represented yet another defeat; and its aftermath – the harassment of left-wing clubs, the imprisonment of radical leaders and the dissolution of the Luxembourg Commission – further angered and alienated Paris radicals and workers. Forty Assembly by-elections on 4 June, mainly occasioned by the multiple candidatures of April, revealed how polarized the electorate had become, not just in Paris but in the provinces as well. In relatively low polls, approximately six moderate republicans as against seven left-wing republicans were elected, with most of the remaining seats going to conservatives. The Seine elected just one moderate republican, but at the same time Proudhon (notorious for his claim that all property is theft) and three other left-wing candidates, and five conservatives, including Thiers, whom three provincial departments also returned. Also successful in the Seine, as well as in three other departments, was Louis Napoleon Bonaparte.

Immediately after the February Revolution Louis Napoleon Bonaparte arrived in Paris from England, where he had lived in exile since his escape in 1846 from imprisonment in the fortress of Ham. On 28 February he wrote a letter to the Provisional Government, announcing his arrival and pledging his support. Having been requested by the Provisional Government to leave France, he obediently returned to London, and enrolled as a special constable to defend the Houses of Parliament during the Chartist demonstration of 10 April. Meanwhile in the National Assembly elections of 23 April three of his cousins gained election, Napoleon Bonaparte (son of Jerome Bonaparte; and Pierre Napoleon Bonaparte (son of Lucien Bonaparte) in Corsica and Lucien Murat (son of Joachim Murat and Caroline Bonaparte) in the Lot. Encouraged by these successes, and by a resurgence of Bonapartism after the February Revolution, partisans of Louis Napoleon Bonaparte put forward his candidature in the by-elections of 4 June, apparently without his prior knowledge or consent, in several departments. The Seine, three provincial departments (Charante-Inférieure, Sarthe and Yonne), and subsequently Corsica as well, elected him. In Le Mans and Paris he attracted considerable working-class support, while in the Yonne and Charante-Inférieure conservatives and peasants voted for him. Since he could appeal both to those who wanted to wage wars of liberation and who were impressed by his interest in poverty and the social question, and to those for whom he represented the army, an ordered society and a conservative and authoritarian state, he could symbolize both the Revolution and the Counter-Revolution. The quadruple election of Louis Napoleon Bonaparte inspired Bonapartist agitation on the streets of Paris and the sudden appearance in Paris of six Bonapartist newspapers. Alarmed, on 12 June the Executive Commission ordered all prefects to arrest Louis Napoleon Bonaparte should he set foot on French territory, and in the Assembly Lamartine, a long-standing opponent of Bonapartism, proposed that an 1832 law of exile should be applied to the Prince. However the next day the Assembly by a large majority rejected this proposal, which had been attacked by Clément Thomas (commander of the Paris National Guard), Louis Blanc and Jules Favre (a moderate republican who had resigned from being Under Secretary at the Ministry of Foreign Affairs on 6 June), and supported only by Ledru-Rollin. Claiming that he did not want to excite disorder, Louis Napoleon Bonaparte sent a letter of resignation to the Assembly, but the government's parliamentary defeat and the public divisions amongst republicans led to widespread rumours that the members of the Executive Commission itself would resign, a course of action which Lamartine and Ledru-Rollin briefly advocated.

The resignation of the Executive Commission was occasioned, not by Bonapartism and Louis Napoleon Bonaparte, but by the Paris National Workshops and the outbreak of a Parisian insurrection on 23 June. The establishment of the Paris National Workshops had been decreed on 26 February by the Provisional Government in response to the unemployment problem in the capital and to the demands of the revolutionary crowds for radical measures. Louis Blanc had advocated that workers in the same trade should be encouraged to set up co-operative workshops with the assistance of state loans, but instead the Provisional Government organized unemployed workers into labour brigades. The number of those enrolled rose remorselessly: by mid-June the total had reached nearly 118,000, equivalent to approximately half the adult male working-class population of Paris. Work projects were never provided for more than about 14,000 of those enrolled; and even the little work on offer mainly took the form of labouring jobs, which were unsuitable for the skilled artisans who constituted a major part of the Parisian work force. Consequently, most of the workers enrolled in the National Workshops remained in an enforced state of idleness. This situation inevitably attracted much criticism. Workers disliked the discipline of the labour brigades, regarded the subsistence wage offered by the National Workshops as inadequate, and resented the absence of sufficient useful and appropriate work. Conservatives, on the other hand, claimed that the National Workshops were too expensive, too unproductive and too dangerous, since they concentrated large numbers of idle workers in Paris at the taxpayers' expense.

The Executive Commission, under pressure from the conservative majority in the National Assembly but at the same time reluctant to abandon completely the Parisian unemployed, planned to scale down the National Workshops while simultaneously creating job opportunities, particularly outside Paris. On 13 May the Executive Commission accepted a proposal from Garnier-Pagès to close enrolment in the National Workshops, and instead invite workers aged between eighteen and twenty-five to enlist in the army. Those who refused were to be sent back to their place of origin. At the same meeting Lamartine suggested replacing the National Workshops with a scheme for the clearance of uncultivated land in France and in Algeria by unemployed workers, who would be paid partly in money and partly in the land they had cleared. The events of 15 May, and the presence of large numbers of workers from the Workshops among the demonstrators, hardened the government's resolve and reinforced conservative fears within the Assembly. On 17 May the Executive Commission repeated to Paris mayors the order to cease enrolments in the National Workshops, though on the same day the Finance Minister, on behalf of the Executive Commission, introduced a bill in the National Assembly for railway nationalization. While the Executive Commission and the Labour Committee of the National Assembly considered the future of the National Workshops in private, public indications of their fate began to emerge. When the relatively conservative Director of the National Workshops, Emile Thomas, resisted such drastic proposals as compulsory army enlistment, he was abruptly dismissed and forced to leave Paris for Bordeaux. His successor, Lalanne, was much less sympathetic to the workers. Shortly afterwards, on 29 May, the dominating figure of the Assembly's Labour Committee, Falloux, in introducing a measure in parliament for the deportation to the provinces of all those enrolled in the National Workshops with less than three months' residence in the department of the Seine, argued that the Workshops encouraged idleness among workers and provided the state with a very poor return for its outlay. The dismissal of Thomas and the comments of Falloux, together with the by-elections of 4 June and the outbreak of Bonapartist agitation, led to renewed popular unrest in Paris at the beginning of June. The Executive Commission responded by further strengthening its military resources in Paris, by forbidding gatherings of armed civilians, and by prosecuting opposition newspapers and political clubs. However, the Executive Commission tempered repression with constructive proposals for tackling the unemployment problem. For instance on 12 June the Minister of Public Works was authorized to spend two million francs on railway-related projects, so as to employ the largest possible number of workers from the National Workshops.

On 16 June the Executive Commission agreed that within five days workers enrolled in the National Workshops and aged between eighteen and twenty-five would have to enlist for two years in the army or be dismissed from the Workshops. As planned, the order was confirmed on 21 June and publicized the next day in *Le Moniteur*. To soften the blow, six million francs were allocated for the completion of the Paris–Lyons railway line on 21 June; and the following day the Executive Commission received a report on agricultural colonies from the Minister of Agriculture and Commerce, while the National Assembly considered a bill for railway nationalization, which Montalembert vigorously opposed. By mid-June at the latest the Executive Commission had decided in effect to close the National Workshops, but it did try to provide jobs for the unemployed through various public works projects and schemes for agricultural colonies and railway nationalization. Due to a lack of resources, and to pressure from the conservative majority in the National Assembly and from individual representatives such as Falloux and Montalembert, those projects and schemes did not materialize and enrolment in the National Workshops was suddenly and drastically curtailed.

After numerous defeats and disappointments, and a succession of parliamentary attacks on the National Workshops, large numbers of Paris workers were thus confronted by the bleak alternatives of army enlistment or immediate loss of all financial support and deportation from the capital. Protests rapidly developed; and, once it became clear that the order on the National Workshops would not be rescinded, a full-scale insurrection erupted throughout the working-class districts of eastern Paris. The total number of insurgents was probably betwen 40,000 and 50,000, whereas enrolment in the National Workshops had reached approximately 118,000, and the adult male working-class population of Paris numbered over 200,000.

The insurgents thus constituted a minority of Paris workers. Against the insurgents were ranged nearly 50,000 regular soldiers and Mobile and Republican Guards, and the Paris National Guard, with a nominal strength of over 200,000 and an effective combatant strength of less than 50,000. In addition, soldiers and National Guardsmen could be summoned from the provinces and, in some cases, deployed quickly by using railway transport. After 23 June had witnessed the erection of hundreds of street barricades and the outbreak of numerous scattered skirmishes and some serious fighting, the National Assembly on 24 June proclaimed martial law in Paris and invested all executive powers in General Cavaignac, who had been appointed supreme commander of all forces in Paris the previous day. Remembering the lessons of February, Cavaignac concentrated his forces and by a series of massive assaults had regained control of the capital by the morning of 26 June. At the outset of the fighting several attempts were made to parley with the rebels but these attempts failed and the insurrection was suppressed with considerable bloodshed. The government forces lost about 1,000 killed, while the insurgents almost certainly suffered a higher casualty rate. The end of the fighting was followed by house-to-house searches for arms and suspected insurgents, the detention of nearly 15,000 suspects, and the transformation of Paris into an armed camp, as thousands of soldiers and Guardsmen filled the capital. At the same time the formal closure of the National Workshops, the suspension of eleven Paris newspapers, and the maintenance of martial law, further emphasized the totality of the insurgents' defect. Altogether the outcome of the June Days seemed to represent an overwhelming victory of the Counter-Revolution over the Revolution.

5   The Bonapartist *Coup d'Etat* of December 1851

The transformation of the Second Republic into the Second Empire between 1848 and 1852 was the astonishing achievement of Louis Napoleon Bonaparte. As late as the summer of 1848 the Bonapartist pretender must have seemed a somewhat marginal figure on the French political stage. As his political opponents gleefully pointed out, he had much to live down – a life spent mainly in exile abroad, acceptance of Swiss citizenship, the inglorious and unsuccessful *coups* at Strasbourg (1836) and Boulogne (1840), participation in the medieval-style Eglinton tournament in Scotland (1839), enrolment as a special constable to defend London against the Chartists (April 1848), even rumours questioning his paternity. On the other hand, he had an unshakeable belief in his own destiny; he had already demonstrated a serious and intelligent interest in politics, military subjects and social problems; and he was the heir to the most charismatic name and legend in French politics. Between 1848 and 1852 Louis Napoleon Bonaparte skilfully exploited the appeal of a reforged Bonapartism and the confusion and division of his political opponents to pursue with resolute determination his goal of re-establishing an imperial Napoleonic régime in France, a goal that he achieved through a remarkable combination of constitutional and unconstitutional acts, and of democratic politics and governmental repression.

The political situation following the June Days in several respects favoured the rise of Louis Napoleon Bonaparte. The June Days demonstrated the isolation of the insurgents and the disunity of the Left. No significant movement in support of the insurgents developed in the provinces; and even in Paris more than half the working-class population did not actively participate in the fighting, while approximately equal numbers of workers fought on the side of the government forces as on the side of the insurgents. In so far as the insurgents had leaders, they were obscure political adventurers such as Pujol. No important left-wing figure or newspaper in France supported the rising, though after its suppression the Left tended to urge clemency and conciliation. The June Days, and, more particularly, exaggerated stories of atrocities, the killings of General Bréa (who had been kidnapped when negotiating with the rebels) and of the Archbishop of Paris (who had attempted to mediate on a barricade), and the fear of further popular violence in Paris, convinced conservatives and even many moderate republicans that the social and constitutional order was threatened more by the revolutionary Left than by the political ambitions of the Bonapartist pretender. In the Assembly conservative representatives continued to form a strong majority, and they had become better organized, having established a caucus known as the Réunion de la Rue de Poitiers to co-ordinate policies. On 28 June the Assembly confirmed the executive authority of General Cavaignac, the commander of the forces that had suppressed the June rising. Cavaignac appointed a government of moderate republicans, which the conservative representatives accepted (apart from forcing the resignation of Carnot as Minister of Public Instruction on 5 July). However, Cavaignac could never rely on majority support in the Assembly, and his government remained in office more or less on sufferance.

During the autumn of 1848 the Assembly debated and finally approved a new constitution for France, a constitution which made it possible for Louis Napoleon Bonaparte to acquire very considerable powers by legal means. Two of the constitution's most important features were the character of the parliament and the character of the presidency. Some representatives, notably Odilon Barrot, wanted a two-chamber legislature, so that the second chamber could serve as a check to any parliamentary or presidential abuse of power. However, a majority in the committee appointed by the Assembly to prepare a draft constitution had recommended a single chamber; and agreement would not have been easily reached as to the composition and role of a second chamber. The Assembly therefore opted for a single chamber. Manhood suffrage and the electoral procedures of April 1848 were retained, though the number of representatives was reduced from 900 to 750.

The constitutional committee had also recommended that the president should be both head of state and prime minister, and should be elected by manhood suffrage. This obviously followed the example of the United States, met the perceived need for a strong executive authority and accorded with the newly orthodox principle of popular sovereignty as expressed by manhood suffrage. By September the opponents of Bonapartism and of Louis Napoleon Bonaparte were beginning to fear the consequences of such a presidency. When Assembly by-elections were held in thirteen departments on 17 September, four departments (Charante-Inférieure, Corsica, Seine and Yonne) re-elected Louis Napoleon Bonaparte. His candidature was also successful in the Moselle and attracted a considerable number of votes in the Nord, Orne and Rhône. This time no attempt was made to prevent his return to France, and he took his seat in the Assembly as a representative of the Seine on 26 September. The plebiscitary nature of the Prince's electoral successes, and the demonstration of his nation-wide appeal in both rural areas and in cities such as Paris and Lyons, confirmed that he would be a formidable candidate in any presidential election by manhood suffrage. Therefore on 6 October Jules Grévy, a moderate republican, introduced an amendment substituting for a president a head of a council of ministers, to be appointed and dismissed at the Assembly's will. The following day the Assembly overwhelmingly rejected the Grévy amendment, and another amendment that there should be a president, though elected by the Assembly rather than by manhood suffrage. The conservative successes in the parliamentary elections of 23 April, and in various local elections between July and September, meant that recourse to manhood suffrage did not alarm the Assembly's conservative majority. Also, Louis Napoleon Bonaparte's initial interventions in the Assembly's proceedings had been so unimpressive as to encourage representatives to underestimate him; and Lamartine on 6 October delivered a powerful speech endorsing the principle of presidential election by the entire electorate. Lingering doubts nevertheless remained. While the Assembly defeated a proposal to review the 1832 law exiling members of former ruling families from France, the Assembly did limit the presidential term of office to four years and did debar any president from serving for a second consecutive term.

Six candidates emerged to fight the presidential election campaign – Louis Napoleon Bonaparte, General Cavaignac, General Changarnier, Lamartine, Ledru-Rollin and Raspail. Lamartine was by now totally discredited, while Changarnier (a Legitimist) and Raspail (a socialist) were both relatively unknown and could appeal only to very small constituencies. Ledru-Rollin stood as a left-wing republican and as such had the support of *La Réforme* and of left-wing republican newspapers in the provinces, and eventually of a more radical Paris newspaper, *La Démocratie pacifique*. He could hope for the votes of skilled artisans and shopkeepers in Paris, in provincial cities such as Marseilles and Lille, and in smaller towns with left-wing traditions, as well as of peasants in the few rural areas in which left-wing republicanism had taken root. However, his appeal was largely restricted to these minority groups, particularly since he was saddled with the conservative-inspired reputation of being a dangerous revolutionary and with at least some of the responsibility for the failures of the Provisional Government and the Executive Commission. Thus it soon became clear that the only serious contenders for the presidency were Cavaignac and Louis Napoleon Bonaparte.

Untypically for a senior career army officer, Cavaignac was a staunch republican, both by family tradition and by personal conviction: his father had been elected to the Convention parliament of 1792; his brother had been a prominent figure in the republican movement before a premature death in 1845; and he himself displayed a firm commitment to a rather limited brand of moderate republicanism. Consequently, *Le National* and other moderate republican newspapers backed him as the defender of the conservative Republic. Most left-wing republicans, socialists and members of the urban working class, of course, hated Cavaignac. They blamed him for the butchery of the June Days and for the severity of the subsequent repression; and they considered that he had betrayed the Republic and the Revolution through his failure to assist foreign nationalist and revolutionary movements and to tackle effectively the domestic problem of urban unemployment. However, left-wing republicans, socialists and urban workers constituted a relatively small proportion of the electorate; and, while the moderate republican constituency was also relatively small, Cavaignac's candidature potentially had a wider appeal. The General had successfully defended the cause of 'order' and 'civilization' during the June Days; he represented existing authority and his election would guarantee a reasonably safe and predictable continuity of government; and the Réunion de la Rue de Poitiers failed to produce a candidate acceptable to most conservatives and capable of winning mass support. Therefore Cavaignac could hope to be the choice of all those who distrusted Bonapartism and Louis Napoleon Bonaparte and who wanted a conservative president and government. A number of factors, though, limited Cavaignac's popularity. Many Catholics opposed the Cavaignac government's educational plans and resented its refusal to help Pope Pius IX restore his authority over the Papal States. Within the élite many conservatives considered that Cavaignac had been too high-handed in suppressing newspapers and in maintaining martial law, and too republican in attempting to prohibit the avoidance of military service through the use of substitutes and in awarding financial compensation to republican victims of the July Monarchy. In addition, Cavaignac lacked both the will and the ability to cultivate influential conservatives and to exploit the administrative machinery of the state to his own electoral advantage. Above all, Cavaignac's identification with the social and administrative *status quo*, with the collection of the 45 centimes tax, and with the continuing depressed state of the economy, heavily penalized him amongst the great mass of peasant voters.

The candidature of Louis Napoleon Bonaparte mixed in a complex manner a glorious legend, a Bonapartist programme and a rejection of the moderate republicanism which had dominated France since the February Revolution. With the passage of time, and with the contrast of the 'inglorious' rulers of France since 1815, images of Napoleon's military victories and of a mighty and orderly French Empire presiding over Continental Europe, had become powerful and persuasive. The Napoleonic legend had been kept alive in many ways: through the memories of those who had served and who remembered the Empire; through numerous publications, prints, songs and forms of memorabilia; through actions of the Orleanist régime, such as the completion of the Arc de Triomphe and the reburial of Napoleon's remains in the Invalides; and through public commemorations, including the funerals of imperial dignatories, the inauguration of statues of Napoleon and of his marshals, and the celebration of Napoleonic anniversaries. As the Bonapartist pretender Louis Napoleon Bonapárte was able to appropriate and exploit this legend to further his own political ambitions. In view of the legend's universal and emotional appeal, this was an enormously valuable asset.

Louis Napoleon Bonaparte also developed a new Bonapartist political programme. In his electoral manifesto of 27 November he presented himself as a symbol of order and security, as a protector of the Catholic Church, as an upholder of the institutions of the family and private property, as a guardian of peace at home and abroad, and as a promoter of national prosperity. Again, such a programme had a universal appeal. Members of the élite who disliked Cavaignac and republicanism saw in Louis Napoleon Bonaparte a conservative candidate who could attract mass support. Catholics, by now generally alienated from the Second Republic, responded to the Prince's promises to restore Catholic schools and the Pope's temporal authority. Peasants, suffering from low agricultural prices and relatively high taxes, welcomed the assurance of tax cuts and the chance to vote against the system. Even urban workers, despairing of republican and socialist remedies for unemployment, turned to the Bonapartist pretender.

The Napoleonic legend and the Bonapartist programme were effectively promoted amongst the electorate. Louis Napoleon Bonaparte's long-standing friend and supporter, Persigny, directed his campaign with the aid of substantial financial resources. Several influential political figures joined the Bonapartist camp, notably Odilon Barrot, Molé, Montalembert and Thiers. While an overall majority of newspapers seem to have been pro-Cavaignac, a large minority declared for the Prince, including several important Paris newspapers (*Le Constitutionnel, L'Evénement, La Gazette de France* and *La Presse*). Also, the majority of voters were peasants, who did not generally read newspapers but who were exposed to various forms of Bonapartist propaganda, particularly at markets and fairs. The parliamentary election of three nephews of Napoleon in April, and Louis Napoleon Bonaparte's own electoral successes in June and September, had already indicated the force of the Bonapartist tide. By 10 and 11 December (the polling days for the presidential election) this tide had become a flood. Louis Napoleon Bonaparte won over five and a half million votes, as against less than one and a half million for Cavaignac and under 400,000 for Ledru-Rollin, the other candidates receiving negligible numbers of votes. Apart from Brittany and Provence, regions with anti-Bonapartist traditions, and the provincial towns of Marseilles and Lille, the candidature of Louis Napoleon Bonaparte swept the board almost everywhere in France, gaining 74 per cent of the votes cast. This astonishing electoral triumph in effect gave Louis Napoleon Bonaparte '*l'élu de six millions*' (the choice of six millions), a popular mandate to begin the task of burying the Second Republic and founding the Second Empire.

While professing to be a republican, from the beginning of his presidency Louis Napoleon Bonaparte in fact began to undermine the Republic. In his electoral manifesto he had disclaimed any imperial ambitions and affirmed his devotion to the Republic, but he had also invoked the memory of the Emperor and promised protection to the Roman Catholic Chúrch. At his inauguration on 20 December he swore an oath of loyalty to the Constitution and informed representatives in the Assembly that they had a great task to accomplish, the founding of the Republic in the interests of all. However, the same day he announced that he had formed a government headed by Odilon Barrot and including the Legitimist Falloux (as Minister of Public Instruction and Religious Affairs), but excluding any republican (apart from Alexandre Bixio, who served for a week as Minister of Agriculture and Commerce). The political intentions and methods of the Prince-President were even more clearly revealed over the Rateau affair. On 28 December Rateau, a conservative representative, introduced a bill for a parliamentary dissolution and new elections. Anxious to secure a more amenable parliament, Louis Napoleon Bonaparte supported the bill, which the Assembly agreed to consider by 470 votes to 337 on 12 January 1849. After this vote, and the conservative character of the Barrot government, had been criticized by left-wing Paris clubs and newspapers, on 26 January the Minister of the Interior proposed in the Assembly the prohibition of political clubs. The rejection of this prohibition by the Assembly, a motion by Ledru-Rollin to impeach the government and anti-government demonstrations in Paris prompted a massive deployment of military force in central Paris on 29 January. In this *coup d'état* atmosphere the Assembly accepted the Rateau bill by a narrow majority of five. Meanwhile Louis Napoleon Bonaparte had adopted a high-profile presidency of a quasi-monarchical character. He took up residence in the Elysée Palace, to which he invited members of the élite to a series of magnificent balls and receptions; he embarked on a round of much-publicized public engagements, such as the opening of new railway lines; and he made presidential visits by special train to provincial towns, where he reviewed army garrisons and National Guard units, attended religious services and official functions, and generally flattered the local inhabitants.

The elections for what became known as the Legislative Assembly were held on 13 May 1849. As in the case of the April 1848 elections, local committees in every department agreed on lists of candidates, lists which were publicized by posters, broadsheets and newspapers. Again, as in April 1848, most of the candidates fell into one of three broad categories, conservative, moderate republican or left-wing republican and socialist. Conservative candidates generally claimed to be the defenders of family, religion and property, the three pillars of the existing social order, against the red menace. In many departments moderate republicans allied with conservatives to fight on the same ticket of social stability and law and order, while emphasizing their commitment to the Republic. On the other hand, left-wing republicans and socialists criticized the Barrot government, particularly its repression of the Left and its decision to send a military expedition to overthrow the Roman Republic, and promised to help workers and peasants by establishing a fairer system of taxation, a free and universal provision of primary education and a guaranteed right to work. In the new Assembly conservatives won approximately 500 seats, moderate republicans eighty and left-wing republicans and socialists 180. In the light of the presidential election results, this represented a rather disappointing performance for the conservatives, a crushing defeat for the moderate republicans and a surprising success for the left-wing republicans and socialists. Conservatives did well in northern and north-western France, but elsewhere were often badly organized. Also, in several departments Bonapartists, Legitimists and Orleanists failed to present a united front, despite the efforts of the Réunion de la Rue de Poitiers to co-ordinate nationally the conservative campaign. Moderate republicans did not project a clear and attractive electoral image, and could not escape from the discredit which their period in power had earned them. Strikingly, virtually all the moderate republicans who had held government posts between February and June 1848 suffered elimination from parliament. In contrast, left-wing republicans and socialists made remarkable gains. Ledru-Rollin came second in the Seine, was elected in four other departments and polled a total of over 700,000 votes. Not only did the Left win seats in Paris and in provincial cities such as Lyons, Lille and Limoges, but also in a considerable number of predominantly rural departments in eastern, central and southern France. This demonstrated the continuing loyalty of many urban workers as well as the success of the Left in penetrating parts of rural France. Thus many peasants, who had voted for Louis Napoleon Bonaparte in December 1848, turned in May 1849 to the Left, which had largely succeeded in carrying off from the Prince-President and the Bonapartists the banner of populist protest.

After the elections of 13 May a crisis rapidly developed over the dispatch of a French military expedition to Rome. At the end of November 1848 popular violence had led to Pope Pius IX fleeing from Rome and seeking exile in the Kingdom of the Two Sicilies.

On 9 February 1849 a newly elected parliamentary assembly proclaimed a republic in the Papal States. Nine days later Pius IX appealed to the Catholic powers to overthrow this republic and restore his authority. Undaunted, the government of the Roman Republic declared that all ecclesiastical property would be confiscated without compensation. Although he had participated in an anti-papal revolt in 1831 and had asserted his commitment to peace in the presidential election campaign, Louis Napoleon Bonaparte hoped that French intervention in support of the Pope would win him personal glory and international prestige. Also, the successful establishment of a radical republic in Rome might have the harmful consequences of encouraging the French Left and of tempting the Austrians to expand into central Italy, particularly after their defeat of the Piedmontese at Novara (23 March 1849); and French Catholics, who had massively voted for Louis Napoleon Bonaparte's presidential candidature, would enthusiastically welcome a papal restoration through French action. These pro-interventionist arguments appealed to Barrot, Drouyn de Lhuys (the Minister of Foreign Affairs) and Falloux, and generally to the Assembly's conservative majority. However the Left, particularly Ledru-Rollin, vigorously opposed what they saw as an attack on a sister republic, an assault on the democratic and nationalist principles of the February Revolution and a breach of the 1848 constitution, which had affirmed that the French Republic would not embark on wars of conquest or use military force against the liberties of any people. Nevertheless, on 16 and 17 April the Assembly voted additional funds for French invervention; on 22 April a military expedition under General Oudinot set sail from Toulon; and on 30 April the French attack on Rome began. The unexpectedly stiff resistance of the Italian republicans, and the parliamentary elections of 13 May, caused a lull in the fighting, but on 3 June Oudinot, who had received reinforcements from France, resumed offensive operations. In the Legislative Assembly Ledru-Rollin on 11 June tabled a motion to impeach the government for having violated the constitution, but this was defeated by 361 votes to 203. Conservatives such as Thiers maintained that the French in Rome were defending the interests of France and civilization, and that the constitution had not been violated since the National Assembly had approved the military budget for the Roman expedition. Ledru-Rollin and his supporters, on the other hand, believed that now the Assembly as well as the government were in breach of the constitution, and that a parliamentary majority had flouted the principles of justice and humanity. On 13 June numerous street demonstrations occurred throughout Paris and a Paris National Guard regiment joined the demonstrators. The mutinous Guardsmen and several left-wing leaders, including Ledru-Rollin, occupied the buildings of a technical college, the Conservatoire des Arts et Métiers, but no popular insurrection developed and the occupants of the Conservatoire soon dispersed to evade arrest.

Most members of the French Left, including many moderate republicans, opposed the Roman expedition, but they did not support armed insurrection. Ledru-Rollin on 12 June, carried away by the passion of parliamentary debate, did declare that the Left would defend the constitution by all possible means, even by force. However, no insurrection was planned for 13 June; the subversion of a National Guard regiment and the occupation of the Conservatoire des Arts et Métiers occurred only after soldiers under General Changarnier had brutally dispersed a peaceful demonstration; and the level of violence is indicated by the relatively low casualty rate of seven deaths. Nevertheless, a popular insurrection might have occurred if the workers of Paris had not been intimidated by memories of the June Days and demoralized by the outbreak of a cholera epidemic; and provincial towns such as Grenoble, Perpignan, Strasbourg and Toulouse, as well as villages and rural communities in several departments, experienced disturbances, while street-fighting in Lyons on 15 June claimed fifty lives. In any case, it suited Louis Napoleon Bonaparte and his government to represent the events of 13 June as a major attempt by the Left to overthrow the Republic by force so as to provide a pretext for a policy of destroying the Left through repression.

Repression of the Left was not a new phenomenon in the history of the Second Republic. A workers' rising in Rouen had been suppressed as early as 27–8 April 1848; in Paris the Left had been under attack since 15 May 1848 and had suffered severely as a result of the June Days; and as soon as he had been elected president Louis Napoleon Bonaparte had begun a political purge of senior official personnel. However, after 13 June 1849 repression of the Left became a systematic and universal feature of government policy. On 13 June itself the Legislative Assembly approved the proclamation of martial law in Paris and the initiation of judicial proceedings against Ledru-Rollin and his associates. The same day a presidential decree suspended six left-wing Paris newspapers, and new restrictive legislation followed on political clubs (19 June 1849) and the newspaper press (27 July 1849). The stifling of all forms of opposition politics and protest was attempted. Radical leaders, left-wing newspapers, workers' clubs and associations, political meetings and banquets, all suffered police and judicial harassment. Shouting radical slogans, singing republican songs and invoking the tradition of France's revolutionary past, could be punished as sedition. Bars and cafés risked closure if they became centres of left-wing debate and propaganda, while dancing, carnivals and festivals could be banned. Gendarmes monitored the movements of migrant workers and other travellers and acted as gatherers of political intelligence. As politically unreliable National Guard units were disbanded and disarmed, the regular army, transformed through reorganization and recomposition into the army of the Prince-President rather than of the Republic, garrisoned the cities and patrolled the countryside, and generally served as an instrument of government repression. Purges of official personnel for political reasons continued and intensified: prefects, sub-prefects, public prosecutors, magistrates, tax collectors, mayors, deputy mayors, university professors, schoolteachers and even postmen, were dismissed, suspended or transferred. The whole political character of France, as well as of the institutions and personnel of the French state, had begun a process of transformation: the forms and symbols of republicanism were exchanged for those of Bonapartism; and the Prince-President lorded it over France like a monarch, holding court in Paris and making regal visits to the provinces.

Many conservatives did not relish the apparently relentless march of Bonapartism and the simultaneous erosion of political liberties. At the same time Louis Napoleon Bonaparte made it clear that he was prepared to act independently of the Assembly's conservative majority by such actions as the formation on 31 October 1849 of a new government composed of ministers more amenable to himself. However, lacking effective leadership and weakened by the divisions among Legitimists and Orleanists, conservatives were in no condition to oppose the Prince-President successfully. Also, the events of 13 June 1849 had confirmed yet again their fears of the Left; the maintenance of order and the gradual recovery of the economy benefited conservative interests; and Catholics, in particular, rejoiced at the French capture of Rome (3 July 1849) and at what became known as the Falloux Law (15 March 1850), which greatly expanded the potential role of the Catholic Church in French education. The Left, of course, attempted to resist. In the Legislative Assembly representatives such as Pierre Leroux consistently opposed government policies, but were consistently out-voted by the conservative majority; and, despite government repression, elements of the French electorate remained surprisingly steadfast in their loyalty to the Left. This was demonstrated by the by-elections of 10 March 1850, when the Left retained eleven seats, and by further by-elections on 28 April 1850, when the left-wing novelist Eugène Sue won in the department of the Seine. These results provoked the government to secure parliamentary approval for a bill disenfranchising all those who paid no personal taxes, who possessed a criminal record and who could not prove three years' consecutive residence in the same canton. Accepted by a parliamentary majority of 433 to 241 on 31 May 1850, the measure deprived almost a third of the electorate of the right to vote, the chief victims coming from the ranks of migrant workers and the urban poor.

An obstacle nevertheless remained in the path of the seemingly irresistible triumph of Louis Napoleon Bonaparte. According to Article 45 of the 1848 constitution, the President was elected for a four-year term of office and was not eligible for re-election until after an interval of four years. Any revision of the constitution required the approval of three-quarters of the representatives in the Assembly. Determined to retain the presidency, Louis Napoleon Bonaparte began to prepare the ground thoroughly. On 3 January 1851 he dismissed General Changarnier from his joint command of the Paris National Guard and of the Paris military garrison. Besides holding these crucially important posts, Changarnier had gained election to the Assembly; and in his capacities as military commander and parliamentary representative he had provided ample evidence of his potential disloyalty. The Assembly reacted to Changarnier's dismissal by passing a vote of no confidence in the government, whereupon Louis Napoleon Bonaparte insisted on the resignation of his ministers. Eventually he formed a new ministerial team, on whose loyalty and obedience he could confidently rely. He then began to mobilize public opinion. From April 1851 a carefully orchestrated campaign resulted in the Assembly being bombarded from the provinces with petitions for constitutional revision. The Assembly itself, after six days of debate, finally voted on 19 July 1851 to approve a revision of the constitution by 446 votes to 278. Conservatives voted massively for revision, but the opposition vote – from left-wing republicans, moderate republicans, some Orleanists and a few Legitimists – was sufficient to deny Louis Napoleon Bonaparte the required three-quarters majority.

Louis Napoleon Bonaparte's failure to secure the required three-quarters majority in the Assembly for constitutional revision meant that he would either have to resign in 1852 or overthrow the constitution by force. His political ambitions and his belief in his own destiny ruled out the possibility of resignation. While he began to prepare for the *coup d'état* by making discreet military dispositions and by yet another ministerial reshuffle (27 October), he also embarked on a clever political manoeuvre. He proposed that the electoral law of 31 May 1850 should be annulled and that manhood suffrage should be restored. Unsurprisingly, the conservative majority in the Assembly rejected this proposal (13 November). This rejection enabled Louis Napoleon Bonaparte to pose as the champion of manhood suffrage and presented the Assembly's conservative majority as opponents of true democracy. In a vote of 17 November the majority in the Assembly made another mistake by failing to assert the right of its president to control the soldiers guarding the parliament buildings.

The *coup d'état* was meticulously planned by a small clique including Saint-Arnaud (Minister of War), Morny (Louis Napoleon Bonaparte's half-brother and future Minister of the Interior) and Maupas (Prefect of Police). Early in the morning of 2 December 1851, the anniversary of Napoleon's coronation (1804) and of his victory of Austerlitz (1805), newspapers and numerous posters announced the dissolution of the Assembly, the restoration of manhood suffrage, the immediate holding of new parliamentary elections, and the proclamation of martial law. Louis Napoleon Bonaparte also issued personal appeals to the people, urging them to approve a new constitution modelled on that of the Consulate if they believed in the France regenerated by the Revolution of 1789 and organized by the Emperor Napoleon, and to the army, emphasizing their indissoluble ties based on shared glories and reverses in the past and on a shared determination to defend France's security and grandeur in the future. At the same time, sixteen parliamentary representatives and sixty-two other potential opponents of the *coup d'état* were arrested and detained; and soldiers occupied the parliament buildings and all important government offices in Paris. Over 200 representatives hurriedly held meetings to organize resistance against the *coup d'état*, only to be promptly arrested and imprisoned as well. On 3 December a handful of representatives still at large tried to incite a popular insurrection, but years of repression, a reluctance to fight for the bourgeois members of a discredited parliament and the overwhelming deployment of military force ensured that popular resistance to the *coup d'état* in Paris was contained and crushed within three days.

While probably less than 2,000 attempted some violent resistance to the *coup d'état* in Paris, perhaps as many as 100,000 did in the provinces. Thirteen departments in central and southern France were particularly affected, notably the Basses-Alpes, Drôme, Gers, Hérault and Var. In those departments thousands of armed peasants and artisans mobilized to protest against the *coup d'état*, to release political prisoners from local jails and to occupy local administration offices. The rebels in the Basses-Alpes even managed to win control of the department's administrative capital and force the prefect to flee. However, within a week units of the regular army had restored order throughout the provinces at the cost of around 100 lives. The incidence of resistance to the *coup d'état* seems to have been the result, not so much of economic factors, as of the degree to which left-wing political ideologies and organizations had penetrated into parts of rural France. Greatly over-reacting to this resistance, the authorities immediately adopted policies of repression on a draconian scale: thirty-one departments were placed under martial law; officials suspected of republican sympathies became the victims of sweeping purges; republican clubs, societies, cafés and newspapers suffered arbitrary closure; and special courts judged nearly 27,000 suspects, of whom about 10,000 received sentences of deportation, mostly to Algeria. In these circumstances a plebiscite was held on 20 December 1851. The entire electorate was asked to confirm Louis Napoleon Bonaparte's authority and his decision to establish a new constitution. Seven and a half million voted yes and only 640,000 no, though about one and a half million voters abstained.

The constitution of Napoleon's Empire served as the model for

Louis Napoleon Bonaparte's constitution of 1852. A Senate, composed of state dignatories, members of the Bonaparte family and life appointees chosen by the Prince-President, examined new legislation and acted as a supreme court. A Council of State of between forty and fifty legal experts, appointed and dismissed by the Prince-President, drafted the texts of all legislative bills. A Legislative Body, elected by manhood suffrage, approved all new legislation and taxation. While very extensive executive authority was vested in the Prince-President, the Legislative Body could not act as an effective democratic institution due to its mode of election, its limited powers, and the enforced secrecy of its parliamentary debates. Finally, on 21 November 1852 in a second plebiscite, the electorate was asked whether or not it approved the re-establishment of the imperial dignity in the person of Louis Napoleon Bonaparte. About 7,800,000 were for with only 250,000 against, though once more a large number of voters abstained (approximately two million). The Second Empire was solemnly proclaimed on 2 December 1852, with Louis Napoleon Bonaparte taking the title of Napoleon III (thus assuming that Napoleon's only legitimate son, the Duke of Reichstadt, had reigned from 1815 until his death in 1832).

Between the overthrow of Napoleon's imperial régime and the founding of the Empire of Napoleon III French history had apparently come full circle. Yet the France of 1852 differed in many important respects from the France of 1815: manhood suffrage, however circumscribed, had become an indelible feature of French politics; the beginnings of universal education, mass literacy and popular newspapers had started to shape a national public opinion; the populations of towns and cities were rapidly increasing, a process soon accompanied by ambitious programmes of urban renewal; the foundation and expansion of banks were helping to create a modern-style capitalist economy; improved communications, particularly railways, encouraged agriculture and industry increasingly to cater to national and international markets; and new technology was transforming the generation of power and the scale of industrial production. At the same time much remained essentially unchanged: most French citizens continued to live in rural areas or small towns and villages, to be directly or indirectly dependent on agriculture for their livelihoods, and to belong to a society dominated by an hereditary land-owning élite; small-scale production characterized most of French manufacturing industry until the end of the century; and the Catholic Church still exercised a powerful influence over the spiritual, educational and social life of the nation. Also, partly because of the brutality of the *coup d'état* and the severity of the subsequent repression, the dynamic of revolution and counter-revolution persisted as a crucial factor in French politics long after 1852.

Notes

1 During the night of 22–23 October 1812 Malet, a republican general involved in an unsuccessful conspiracy in 1808, escaped from his confinement, announced that Napoleon had died in Russia, and with a small band of conspirators took command of units of the Paris National Guard and seized control of the civil administration of the capital. However, the bulk of the Paris military garrison and its commander remained loyal to Napoleon, and within a week Malet and his accomplices had been tried and executed. Nevertheless Napoleon was so alarmed that he abandoned his retreating army in Russia in order to reassert his authority personally in Paris.

2 G. de Bertier de Sauvigny, *La Restauration*, Paris, 1974, p. 459.

3 See E. Hennet de Goutel (ed.), *Mémoires du général marquis Alphonse d'Hautpoul, paire de France, 1789–1865*, Paris, 1906, p. 184; J. F. F. La Roche, *Souvenirs d'un officier de gendarmerie sous la Restauration*, Paris, 1914, pp. 185–6.

4 J. L. L. Blanc, *Révolution française. Histoire de dix ans, 1830–1840*, 5 vols, Paris, 1841–4, vol. I, pp. 189–452, vol. II, pp. 33–6; A. Delvau, *Histoire de la Révolution de février*, Paris, 1850, pp. 37–57. For the references to de Tocqueville and Marx see the Guide to Further Reading.

5 D. H. Pinkney, *The French Revolution of 1830*, Princeton, 1972, p. 195, n. 78, and pp. 252–73.

6 'The allies of the *chouans* [royalist opponents of the Revolution in the Vendée] and the admirers of Robespierre and Marat' [prominent figures in the extreme republican phase of the Revolution, 1793–4]; Proclamation of the Prefect of Police (*Le Moniteur universel*, 7 June 1832, p. 1295).

7 The principal radical banquets were those held at Le Mans (10 August 1847), Strasbourg (5 September 1847), Autun (27 October 1847), Lille (7 November 1847), Dijon (21 November 1847), Chalon (19 December 1847) and Limoges (2 January 1848). Left-wing speakers at these and other banquets included Louis Blanc, Victor Considérant, Garnier-Pagès and Ledru-Rollin.

8 P. H. Amann, *Revolution and Mass Democracy: The Paris Club Movement in 1848*, Princeton, 1975, p. 98.

Guide to Further Reading

Agulhon, M. 1973: *The Republican Experiment, 1848–1852*. Cambridge University Press.

Amann, P. H. 1975: *Revolution and Mass Democracy: The Paris Club Movement in 1848*. Princeton University Press.

Berenson, E. G. 1984: *Populist Religion and Left-Wing Politics in France, 1830–1852*. Princeton University Press.

Bertier de Sauvigny, G. de. 1966: *The Bourbon Restoration*. Pennsylvania University Press.

Bury, J. P. T. 1985: *France, 1814–1940*. Methuen.

Bury, J. P. T. and Tombs, R. P. 1986: *Thiers, 1797–1877: A Political Life*. Allen & Unwin.

Calman, A. 1980: *Ledru-Rollin and the Second French Republic*. Octagon Books.

Cobban, A. 1970: *A History of Modern France*, vol. 2. *1799–1871*. Penguin Books.

Collins, I. 1959: *The Government and the Newspaper Press in France, 1814–1881*. Oxford University Press.

De Luna, F. A. 1969: *The French Republic under Cavaignac: 1848*. Princeton University Press.

Fortescue, W. 1983: *Alphonse de Lamartine: A Political Biography*. Croom Helm.

Howarth, T. E. B. 1961: *Citizen-King: The Life of Louis-Philippe, King of the French*. Eyre & Spottiswoode.

Jardin, A. and Tudesq, A. J. 1983: *Restoration and Reaction, 1815–1848*. Cambridge University Press.

Jennings, L. C. 1973: *France and Europe in 1848: A Study of French Foreign Affairs in time of Crisis*. Clarendon Press.

Johnson, D. 1963: *Guizot: Aspects of French History, 1787–1874*. Routledge & Kegan Paul.

Mackenzie, N. 1982: *The Escape from Elba: The Fall and Flight of Napoleon, 1814–1815*. Oxford University Press.

Magraw, R. 1983: *France, 1815–1914: The Bourgeois Century*. Fontana Paperbacks.

Mansel, P. 1981: *Louis XVIII*. Blond & Briggs.

Margadant, T. W. 1979: *French Peasants in Revolt: The Insurrection of 1851*. Princeton University Press.

Marx, K. 1977: *The Class Struggles in France: 1848 to 1850* and *The Eighteenth Brumaire of Louis Bonaparte* in *Surveys from Exile*, vol. 2. Penguin Books.

Merriman, J. M. (ed.) 1975: *1830 in France*. New Viewpoints.

Merriman, J. M. 1978: *The Agony of the Republic: The Repression of the Left in Revolutionary France, 1848–1851*. Yale University Press.

Pinkney, D. H. 1972: *The French Revolution of 1830*. Princeton University Press.

Pinkney, D. H. 1986: *Decisive Years in France, 1840–1847*. Princeton University Press.

Price, R. 1972: *The French Second Republic: A Social History*. Batsford.

Price, R. (ed.) 1975: *Revolution and Reaction: 1848 and the Second French Republic*. Croom Helm.

Price, R. 1983: *The Modernization of Rural France: Communications Networks and Agricultural Market Structures in Nineteenth-Century France*. Hutchinson.

Richardson, N. 1966: *The French Prefectoral Corps, 1814–1830*. Cambridge University Press.

Thompson, J. M. 1965: *Louis Napoleon and the Second Empire*. Basil Blackwell.

Tocqueville, A. de 1987: *Recollections*. Transaction Books.

Traugott, M. 1985: *Armies of the Poor: Determinants of Working-Class Participation in the Parisian Insurrection of June 1848*. Princeton University Press.

Tudesq, A. J. 1964: *Les Grands Notables en France, 1840–1849: Etude historique d'une psychologie sociale*, 2 vols. Presses universitaires de France.

Tudesq, A. J. 1965: *L'Election présidentielle de Louis-Napoléon Bonaparte, 10 décembre 1848*. A. Colin.

Index

Prussia, 2, 6, 13–14
Pujol, Louis, 71

Quatre-Bras, 11
Quinet, Edgar, 54

Rambouillet, 30
Raspail, François, 66, 73
Rateau, Jean Pierre Lamotte, 76
reform banquet campaign (1847–8), 49–50, 52, 54, 56, 84
Réforme, La, 44, 56, 73
Reichstadt, Duke of (King of Rome), 5, 9, 83
Republican Guard, 61, 70
Réunion de la Rue de Poitiers, 72, 74, 77
Revue du progrès, La, 44
Revue indépendante, La 44
Rheims, 21, 32
Rhine, Confederation of the, 2
Rhineland, 6
Rhône, department of the, 72
Richelieu, Duke of, 18–19
Robespierre, Maximilien, 34, 43
Roman Catholic Church, 4, 8, 14, 16–17, 19–21, 25, 32, 37, 63, 64, 75–6, 80, 83
Roman Republic, 77–8
Rome, 2, 77–8, 80
Rome, King of (Duke of Reichstadt), 5, 9, 83
Roubaix, 39
Rouen, 14, 39, 57, 65, 79
Rousseau, Jean Jacques, 19
Rue Transnonain, massacre of the, 43, 55
Russia, 2, 7, 13–14, 46

Saint-Arnaud, General, 81
Saint-Cloud, palace of, 29
St Etienne, 39
St Germain-en-Laye, 39
Saint-Germain-l'Auxerrois, 41
St Helena, 13, 40
St Lucia, island of, 7
Saint Ouen, proclamation of, 6
Salvandy, Count of, 36
Sand, George, 44
Sardinia, 6
Sarthe, department of the, 67
Savoy, 6, 7, 13
Saxony, 6
Schönbrunn, treaty of, 3
Sébastiani, Viscount, 34
Seine, department of the, 17, 38, 62–4, 66–7, 69, 72–3, 77, 80

September press laws (1835), 44, 59
Sète, 39
Sobrier, Joseph, 65–6
Société des amis de la liberté de la presse, 23
Society of the Rights of Man, 43
Society of the Seasons, 45
Soult, Marshal, 36, 46–7
Spain, 2, 20, 22, 48
Strasbourg, 15, 39, 44–5, 71, 79
Sue, Eugène, 80
Sweden, 5
Switzerland, 2, 6, 7, 35, 44, 48

Tahiti, 48
Talleyrand, Prince of, 5
Temps, Le, 25
Thiers, Adolphe, 27, 30, 34, 36, 46, 48, 51, 56, 66, 75, 78
Thomas, Clément, 67
Thomas, Emile, 68–9
Tobago, island of 7
Tocqueville, Alexis de, 33, 36, 66
Toulon, 12, 78
Toulouse, 12, 41, 79
Tours, 39
Trafalgar, battle of, 2
Treaties of 1814, 6–7
Treaties of 1815, 13–14, 42, 48
Tribune, La, 43–4
Tribune des Départements, La, 25
Trinidad, island of, 7
Tuileries Palace, 8, 10, 29, 51, 55

United Netherlands, 1, 6

Var, department of the, 82
Vendée, 3, 10, 25, 41–2
Venetia, 6, 13
Versailles, 39
Versailles, palace of, 8, 40
Victoria, Queen, 48
Vienna, Congress of, 11
Villèle, Count of, 20–3
Villemain, François, 36
Vincennes, 36
Voltaire, 19

Warsaw, Grand Duchy of, 2
Waterloo, battle of, 11–13, 25, 45, 47
Wellington, Duke of, 2, 8
Westphalia, 2, 6
Wolowski, François, 65

Yonne, department of the, 67, 72